M·E·N·U · M·A·S·T·E·R·S

QUICK & EASY MEALS

EDITED BY
JENNI TAYLOR

OCTOPUS BOOKS

MENU MATCH CODE
To allow more flexibility within the menus we have added
bold numbers after certain recipes to offer suitable
alternatives.
Thus, if the numbers ·3·11·14· appear after a starter, they
indicate that the starter of Menu 3, 11, or 14 could be
substituted.
Using the MENU MATCH CODE you will be sure to find
a menu to suit all tastes.

NOTES
Standard spoon measurements are used in all recipes
1 tablespoon – one 15 ml spoon
1 teaspoon – one 5 ml spoon
All spoon measures are level
Where amounts of salt and pepper are not specified, the
cook should use her own discretion.
Canned foods should not be drained, unless so stated in the
recipe. For all recipes, quantities are given in metric,
imperial and American measures. Follow one set of
measures only, because they are not interchangeable.

Jacket photograph: Beef Steaks with Orange, Salad Nicoise

First published 1986 by
Octopus Books Limited
59 Grosvenor Street, London W 1

© 1986 Octopus Books Limited

ISBN 0 7064 2543X

Produced by Mandarin Publishers Ltd
22a Westlands Rd
Quarry Bay, Hong Kong
Printed in Hong Kong

C · O · N · T · E · N · T · S

I·N·T·R·O·D·U·C·T·I·O·N

Menu Masters 'Quick and Easy Meals' is designed to take the anguish out of menu-planning. It is especially for those whose time is limited but who none the less like to entertain with style, serving interesting and appetizing food.

The menus have been compiled to match every occasion and everyone's pocket from celebration dinners to casual suppers, barbecues to brunches. Most of the meals can be ready to serve within an hour. So if you want to conjure up an impressive dinner when you get home from work or quickly satisfy a hungry family after a day in the country, there will be a menu to suit. The menu match numbers at the end of the recipes can be used to create even more delicious combinations.

The introduction to each menu gives useful cookery hints and tips, plus wine notes, and, if you have time to spare, extra finishing touches for table settings.

The detailed countdowns will make sure nothing is forgotten and speed you on to serving time.

If quick and easy meals are your style of entertaining, the secret is to have a storecupboard well-stocked with quality convenience foods. Keep last minute shopping to a minimum, only the fresh ingredients should be required.

Quick and Easy Meals shows you how to make clever short cuts to ensure your family and friends will be suitably impressed by the speed and efficiency of your culinary expertise.

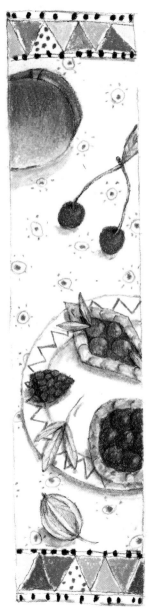

△ M·E·N·U △

· 1 ·

Summer Dinner for 4

Peppered Liver Pâté

·

Beef Stroganoff
Buttered New Potatoes

·

Hot Bacon and Banana Salad

·

Blackcurrant Fluff

This summer dinner menu takes just 1 hour to put together and will impress even the most critical of guests, proving that it's the quality of ingredients that counts, rather than the time it takes to prepare a meal.

Making Melba Toast

Serve the Peppered Liver Pâté, flavoured with green peppercorns, with Melba toast. Melba toast can be bought, but better still make your own. Remove the crusts from slices of packet sliced bread and toast the bread on both sides. Using a sharp knife, cut each slice in two horizontally then place the bread slices on a baking sheet and pop in a moderate or hot oven until the toast has dried. This is an excellent way of using up stale bread; save on fuel by baking the toast when you are using the oven for something else. Melba toast keeps well if stored in an airtight container.

Hospitality

Welcome your guests with a pre-dinner aperitif but don't fill them with salted peanuts, crisps or crackers. If splashing out and serving two wines, choose white for the pâté and red with the Stroganoff.

Q · U · I · C · K · & · E · A · S · Y

Peppered Liver Paté

Metric/Imperial	American
125 g/4 oz butter	½ cup butter
2 rashers streaky bacon, rinded and chopped	2 slices fatty bacon, rinded and chopped
1 onion, chopped	1 onion, chopped
1 clove garlic, peeled and crushed	1 clove garlic, peeled and crushed
125 g/4 oz mushrooms, sliced	1 cup sliced mushrooms
250 g/8 oz chicken livers, cleaned and roughly chopped	1 cup chicken livers, firmly packed, cleaned and roughly chopped
sprig of fresh thyme or pinch of dried thyme	sprig of fresh thyme or pinch of dried thyme
1 bay leaf	1 bay leaf
1-2 tablespoons brandy	1-2 tablespoons brandy
3 tablespoons green peppercorns	3 tablespoons green peppercorns
salt	salt
sprigs of thyme, to garnish	sprigs of thyme, to garnish

1. Melt 50 g/2 oz (¼ cup) of the butter in a frying pan (skillet) and sauté the bacon, onion, garlic, mushrooms, livers and herbs, stirring occasionally, for 10 minutes or until cooked.

2. Spoon into a blender or food processor with the pan juices and the brandy, discarding the bay leaf, and blend until smooth.

3. Stir in 2 tablespoons of the green peppercorns, and season. Spoon into four serving dishes and smooth the top.

4. Clarify the remaining butter by heating it until it foams, then straining through muslin (cheesecloth).

5. Sprinkle the remaining green peppercorns over the surface of the pâté and pour over the melted clarified butter. Small sprigs of thyme may be arranged on top before pouring over the clarified butter. Chill until set. Serve with Melba toast.
·4·10·14·

Beef Stroganoff

Metric/Imperial	American
50 g/2 oz butter	¼ cup butter
1 medium Spanish onion, sliced	1 medium Spanish onion, sliced
125 g/4 oz mushrooms, sliced	1 cup sliced mushrooms
150 ml/¼ pint red wine	⅔ cup red wine
1 teaspoon German mustard	1 teaspoon German mustard
150 ml/¼ pint soured cream	⅔ cup sour cream
½ teaspoon caraway seeds	½ teaspoon caraway seeds
pinch of sugar	pinch of sugar
salt	salt
freshly ground black pepper	freshly ground black pepper
750 g/1½ lb fillet or sirloin steak, cut into strips	1½ lb filet mignon or sirloin steak, cut into strips

1. Melt one third of the butter in a saucepan and gently sauté the onion for 5 minutes until soft and lightly coloured.

2. Push the onion to one side of the pan. Melt a further third of the butter in the pan, add the mushrooms and stir to coat.

3. Add the wine, cover the pan and simmer for about 10 minutes or until almost all the liquid is absorbed. Stir in the mustard, soured cream, caraway seeds, sugar, and salt and pepper to taste. Heat through gently, but do not allow to boil.

4. Melt the remaining butter in a large frying pan (skillet) and sauté the steak strips for 2 minutes on each side for fillet steak and 3 minutes for sirloin.

5. Transfer the steak strips to a warm serving dish, pour over the sauce and serve accompanied by Buttered New Potatoes. Serve the salad to follow.
·4·10·12·

Hot bacon and banana salad

Buttered New Potatoes

Metric/Imperial	American
750 g/1½ lb small new potatoes	1½ lb small new potatoes
salt	salt
50 g/2 oz butter	¼ cup butter
freshly ground black pepper	freshly ground black pepper
2 tablespoons chopped parsley	2 tablespoons chopped parsley

1. Scrub the potatoes. Cook in a saucepan of boiling salted water for 10 to 15 minutes or until tender.
2. Toss in the butter, salt, pepper and parsley.

Hot Bacon and Banana Salad

Metric/Imperial	American
250 g/8 oz bean sprouts	½ lb bean sprouts
175 g/6 oz mangetouts,	1 cup snow peas
1 bunch of watercress, divided into sprigs	1 bunch of watercress, divided into sprigs
2 bananas, sliced	2 bananas, sliced
juice of 2 lemons	juice of 2 lemons
juice of 2 oranges	juice of 2 oranges
1 tablespoon olive oil	4 slices lean bacon, chopped
4 rashers lean bacon, chopped	grated rind of 1 lemon
grated rind of 1 lemon	1 clove garlic, peeled and finely chopped
1 clove garlic, peeled and finely chopped	1 tablespoon chopped tarragon
1 tablespoon chopped tarragon	salt
salt	freshly ground black pepper
freshly ground black pepper	1 tablespoon chopped pistachio nuts
1 tablespoon chopped pistachio nuts	

1. Mix the bean sprouts, mangetouts and watercress sprigs together in a salad bowl.
2. Toss the sliced bananas in half the lemon and orange juice and add to the salad bowl.

3. Heat the oil in a frying pan (skillet) and sauté the chopped bacon until it crisps slightly.

4. Stir in the remaining lemon juice, the lemon rind, garlic and tarragon, and simmer for 30 seconds. Add salt and pepper to taste.

5. Spoon over the salad ingredients, add the pistachio nuts and toss quickly together. Serve immediately. ·2·9·

Blackcurrant Fluff

Metric/Imperial	American
1 × 425 g/15 oz can blackcurrants	1 × 1 lb can black currants
grated rind and juice of 1 medium orange	grated rind and juice of 1 medium orange
15 g/1/2 oz gelatine	1 tablespoon gelatin
2 egg whites	2 egg whites
50 g/2 oz caster sugar	1/4 cup sugar
whipped cream, to decorate	whipped cream, to decorate
sponge fingers or macaroons, to serve	lady fingers or macaroons, to serve

1. Place the blackcurrants with their syrup and half the orange rind in a blender or food processor and blend to a purée.

2. Dissolve the gelatine in the orange juice in a bowl set over hot water. Stir into the blackcurrant purée. Chill until on the point of setting.

3. Whisk the egg whites to soft peaks, then whisk in the sugar a little at a time until thick and glossy. Fold into the blackcurrant mixture.

4. Spoon the mixture into four individual dishes and chill until required.

5. Instead of simply chilling the mixture before serving, pop the four individual dishes of Blackcurrant Fluff into the freezer for 30 minutes before serving. The result – a delicious iced desert.

6. Decorate with whipped cream and the remaining orange rind. Serve with sponge (lady) fingers or macaroons. ·5·

To serve at 8 pm:

6.00: Open the red wine. Set the table. Chill the white wine, if using.

7.00: Prepare the Peppered Liver Pâté, spoon into individual serving dishes, top with clarified butter and refrigerate. Make the Melba Toast.

7.15: Prepare the Blackcurrant Fluff, pour into individual dishes and refrigerate.

7.30: Scrub the new potatoes. Clean and prepare the vegetables for the salad and toss the banana in lemon juice; arrange in the salad bowl. Fry the chopped bacon until crisp and make up the dressing.

7.40: Boil the potatoes. Prepare the Beef Stroganoff, pouring over the sauce just before serving.

8.00: Drain the new potatoes, toss in a little butter and chopped parsley. Keep warm. Serve the pâté with the Melba toast.

Between courses: Toss the salad with the hot dressing. Whip the cream for the dessert and decorate.

F · R · E · E · Z · E · R · N · O · T · E · S

Pack and freeze the Peppered Liver Pâté at the end of stage 3. Thaw overnight in the refrigerator. Finish as per recipe.

Cook's Tip:

Pop the Blackcurrant Fluff into the freezer for 30 minutes before serving for a delicious iced dessert.

Optional Extra:

Instead of filling up your guests with salty snacks, serve a selection of fresh vegetable crudites and olives. These will whet their appetites rather than dull their palates.

For four people prepare approximately 500 g/1 lb of vegetables and make the selection as varied as possible. Carrots, peppers, cauliflower and mushrooms will produce a colourful platter.

Keep the dips simple. But a good quality hummus, or taramasalata from the local delicatessen, or flavour a small carton of natural yogurt with crushed garlic and chopped chives.

△ M·E·N·U △

· 2 ·

Barbecue for 4

Avocado Dip

·

Barbecued Lamb Kebabs
Corn and Pasta Salad
Orange and Celery Salad
Garlic and Cheese Bread

·

Cherries in Red Wine

When cooking over a barbecue it is vital to light it well in advance. The coals should be white rather than red hot before you start to cook — this could take up to 45 minutes to achieve. Position the barbecue down-wind of where your guests will be standing so that they are not plagued by smoke, and keep a jug of warm water at the ready to damp down any flames.

Barbecue Food

The economical Barbecued Lamb Kebabs recipe makes a little expensive meat go a long way and is perfect to serve at a barbecue.

There is nothing like the smell of food cooking over coals to stimulate the appetite, so it is important to serve nibbles or a starter that your guests can keep tucking into. This Avocado Dip is a perfect start to a meal, especially if you serve it with plenty of crudités — raw vegetables cut into bite-sized pieces — such as baby radishes, carrot and cucumber sticks, spring onions (scallions), raw button mushrooms, strips of red and green pepper. Alternatively serve a selection of savoury crackers and Melba toast (see page 5).

Avocado Dip

Metric/Imperial
1 small ripe avocado,
  peeled and chopped
1 clove garlic, peeled
1 × 100 g/3½ oz can or
  jar smoked cod's roe,
  drained
juice of ½ lemon
1 tablespoon olive oil
salt
freshly ground black pepper

American
1 small ripe avocado,
  peeled, pitted and
  chopped
1 clove garlic, peeled
1 × 3½ oz can or jar
  smoked cod's roe, drained
juice of ½ lemon
1 tablespoon olive oil
salt
freshly ground black pepper

1. Put all the ingredients, with salt and pepper to taste, into a blender or food processor. Blend until smooth. Cover and chill before serving.
2. Serve with crudités or Melba toast (see page 5).

Barbecued lamb kebabs served on a bed of boiled rice.

Barbecued Lamb Kebabs

Metric/Imperial
½ shoulder of lamb, boned
  and cubed
1 small green pepper, cored,
  seeded and cut into 8
  pieces
2 lambs' kidneys, skinned,
  cored and halved
2 onions, quartered
4 tomatoes, halved
4 mushrooms, halved
Marinade:
2 tablespoons olive oil
2 tablespoons wine vinegar
pinch of dried mixed herbs
pinch of sugar
pinch of dry mustard
1 clove garlic, crushed
boiled rice, to serve

American
1 lb boned square-cut
  shoulder lamb, cubed
1 small green pepper, seeded
  and cut into 8 pieces
2 lamb kidneys, skinned,
  cored and halved
2 onions, quartered
4 tomatoes, halved
4 mushrooms, halved
Marinade:
2 tablespoons olive oil
2 tablespoons wine vinegar
pinch of dried mixed herbs
pinch of sugar
pinch of dry mustard
1 clove garlic, peeled and
  crushed
boiled rice, to serve

1. Put the lamb cubes into a bowl. Mix the marinade ingredients together and pour over the lamb. Leave in a cool place, turning occasionally.
2. Thread the lamb, green pepper, kidneys, onion, tomatoes and mushrooms onto four skewers and baste with the marinade.
3. Place over the barbecue or under a preheated hot grill (broiler) and cook, turning frequently, until tender. Transfer to a warm serving plate with the boiled rice and serve. ·4·13·

Corn and Pasta Salad

Metric/Imperial	American
250 g/8 oz pasta shells	1/2 lb pasta shells
salt	salt
3 tablespoons olive oil	3 tablespoons olive oil
1 tablespoon wine vinegar	1 tablespoon wine vinegar
1 × 198 g/7 oz can tuna	1 × 7 oz can tuna
1 teaspoon grated lemon rind	1 teaspoon grated lemon rind
1 clove garlic, peeled and crushed	1 clove garlic, peeled and crushed
2 celery sticks, sliced	2 celery stalks, sliced
1 onion, thinly sliced	1 onion, thinly sliced
1 × 198 g/7 oz can sweetcorn, drained	1 × 7 oz can whole kernel corn, drained
freshly ground black pepper	freshly ground black pepper
chopped parsley, to garnish	chopped parsley, to garnish

1. Cook the pasta shells in a large saucepan of boiling salted water for 10 minutes until tender but al dente. Drain and cool.
2. Put the oil and wine vinegar into a bowl. Add the oil from the tuna, the lemon rind and garlic and stir well.
3. Flake the tuna and add to the oil mixture with the celery, onion, corn and pasta shells. Toss together well to combine all ingredients, adding salt and pepper to taste. Chill before serving. Garnish with chopped parsley. ·3·7·8·

Orange and Celery Salad

Metric/Imperial	American
4 oranges, peeled and separated into segments	4 oranges, peeled and separated into segments
1 head of celery, finely sliced	1 head celery, finely sliced
1 mild onion, coarsely chopped	1 mild onion, coarsely chopped
1 teaspoon coriander seeds, lightly crushed	1 teaspoon coriander seeds, lightly crushed
Dressing:	Dressing:
2 tablespoons red wine vinegar or lemon juice	2 tablespoons red wine vinegar or lemon juice
5 tablespoons olive oil	5 tablespoons olive oil
salt	salt
freshly ground black pepper	freshly ground black pepper
celery leaves, to garnish	celery leaves, to garnish

1. Remove any pith or membrane from the orange segments and place in a salad bowl with the celery and onion. Fork through lightly to mix. Sprinkle with the coriander seeds.
2. Combine all the dressing ingredients and whisk together with a fork to blend thoroughly. Pour over the salad, toss gently and garnish with celery leaves. ·3·7·8·

Garlic and Cheese Bread

Metric/Imperial	American
1 small French stick loaf	1 small French stick loaf
25 g/1 oz butter, softened	2 tablespoons softened butter
75 g/3 oz full-fat soft cheese, softened	1/3 cup full-fat curd cheese, softened
2 cloves garlic, peeled and crushed	2 cloves garlic, peeled and crushed
salt	salt
freshly ground black pepper	freshly ground black pepper

1. Split the French stick in half lengthways. Spread

the cut surfaces on both halves with butter.

2. Beat the cheese with the garlic and salt and pepper to taste. Spread one half of the French stick with the cheese mixture and sandwich together with the other half. Wrap in foil.

3. Heat the French stick over the barbecue, turning often, or bake in a preheated oven (190°C/375°F), Gas Mark 5 for 10 minutes. Serve piping hot.

Variation:

Any soft cheese such as Blue Brie, Boursin or Camembert, could be used for the Garlic and Cheese Bread.

Cherries in Red Wine

Metric/Imperial

500 g/1 lb red or black cherries, stoned
300 ml/½ pint light red wine
4 tablespoons sugar
½ teaspoon ground cinnamon
2 teaspoons cornflour
4 tablespoons redcurrant jelly
vanilla ice cream, to serve

American

1 lb red or bing cherries, pitted
1¼ cups light red wine
4 tablespoons sugar
½ teaspoon ground cinnamon
2 teaspoons cornstarch
4 tablespoons red currant jelly
vanilla ice cream, to serve

1. Place the cherries, wine, sugar and cinnamon in a saucepan. Bring slowly to the boil.

2. Mix the cornflour and redcurrant jelly together. Stir into the cherries and simmer for 1 minute. Remove from the heat, cover and leave for 5 minutes.

3. Serve warm or cold, with vanilla ice cream. If a thicker sauce is desired, remove the cherries and reduce the liquid further.

Variation:

Canned strawberries or raspberries can be used instead of blackcurrants. If the mixture is too sweet, add the grated rind of 1 large lemon and 1 tablespoon of lemon juice.

On the day:

Cube the lamb and leave to marinate as soon as possible.

To serve at 12.30 pm:

10.30: Open the red wine, if using. Arrange the barbecue, table and chairs etc, in the garden.

11.00: Prepare the Avocado Dip, transfer to a serving bowl, cover and refrigerate. Prepare the vegetable crudités, if using, cover and refrigerate.

11.15: Cook the pasta for the Corn and Pasta Salad, and prepare the remaining ingredients. Drain the pasta, make up the salad and refrigerate.

11.30: Prepare the salad ingredients and dressing for the Orange and Celery Salad but do not pour the dressing over.

11.40: Prepare the kebab (kabob) vegetables. Drain the lamb and assemble the kebabs.

11.50: Light the barbecue. Make the Garlic and Cheese Bread, wrap in foil and set aside.

12.00: Prepare the Cherries in Red Wine. If you are planning to serve them warm, reheat for a few minutes before serving. Make up the punch, if using.

About 12.20: Put the kebabs on the barbecue. Add the dressing to the Orange and Celery Salad. Serve the Avocado Dip with crudités or Melba toast.

Between courses: Put the bread on the barbecue 10 minutes before serving the kebabs. Take the ice cream out of the freezer a little in advance to soften.

Rescue Tactic:

If the weather turns cold or rainy the kebabs can be cooked under a hot grill. Preheat the grill for 10 minutes. Cook the kebabs for 4 to 5 minutes on each side basting with the marinade as they cook. Heat the Garlic and Cheese Bread in a hot oven (190°C/ 375°F), Gas Mark 5 for 10 minutes.

F·R·E·E·Z·E·R · N·O·T·E·S

Cool, pack and freeze the Cherries in Red Wine at the end of stage 2. Thaw overnight in the refrigerator. Reheat gently if wished.

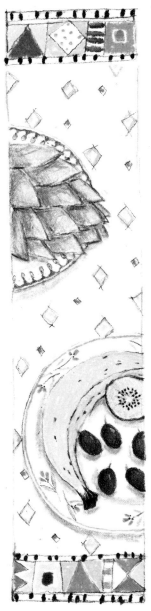

△ M · E · N · U △

· 3 ·

Lunch on the Lawn for 4

Gazpacho

·

Sprouting Chicken Salad
Dressed Avocado
Spicy Tomatoes
Hot Cheese and Anchovy Bread

·

Strawberry and Cointreau Crush

This tempting summer lunch menu is perfect for outside eating and can be prepared well in advance if necessary. (The avocados are the one exception, because they discolour on standing – so slice just before serving.)

Chilled Soup

Gazpacho is a very traditional summer soup from Spain and is always popular, even with those who tend to turn up their noses at the thought of a chilled soup. Make plenty of the tasty hot Cheese and Anchovy Bread to serve with both the Gazpacho and the salad.

Summer Drinks

Serve a chilled white wine, such as a German Piesporter, or try this summery White Wine Cup. Finely slice 1 orange and 1 lemon and place in a punch bowl or large jug. Pour over 4 tablespoons brandy and leave to soak for about 30 minutes. Just before serving, add 1 litre/1¾ pints (4 cups) well-chilled dry white wine. Dilute the mixture with about 500 ml/18 fl oz (2 cups) lemonade or soda water.

Gazpacho

Metric/Imperial	American
1 large onion, chopped	*1 large onion, chopped*
1 cucumber, peeled and chopped	*1 cucumber, peeled and chopped*
1 green pepper, cored, seeded and chopped	*1 green pepper, seeded and chopped*
1 clove garlic, peeled and chopped	*1 clove garlic, peeled and chopped*
450 g/1 lb tomatoes, peeled, seeded and chopped	*2 cups peeled, seeded and chopped tomatoes*
1 tablespoon chopped parsley	*1 tablespoon chopped parsley*
1 tablespoon chopped mint	*1 tablespoon chopped mint*
few almonds or hazelnuts (optional)	*few almonds or hazelnuts (optional)*
1 tablespoon olive oil	*1 tablespoon olive oil*
1 tablespoon wine vinegar	*1 tablespoon wine vinegar*
1/2 teaspoon salt	*1/2 teaspoon salt*
freshly ground white pepper	*freshly ground white pepper*
1 litre/1 3/4 pints water	*4 cups water*
To Garnish:	To Garnish:
1 onion, finely diced	*1 onion, finely diced*
1/4 cucumber, peeled and finely diced	*1/4 cucumber, peeled and finely diced*
1 red or green pepper, cored, seeded and finely diced	*1 red or green pepper, cored, seeded and finely diced*
12 olives, stoned and sliced	*12 pitted olives, sliced*

1. Put all the ingredients, except the water and garnishes, into a blender or food processor and blend at the lowest speed for about 1 minute or until smooth. Alternatively, pound these ingredients together, using a pestle and mortar.
2. Pour into a large serving bowl and stir in the water. Cover the gazpacho and chill well before serving.
3. When ready to serve, ice cubes may be added. Serve the garnish ingredients separately in small bowls. ·4·8·

Sprouting Chicken Salad

Metric/Imperial	American
1 cooked chicken, about 1.5 kg/3 lb	*1 cooked chicken, about 3 lb*
2 tablespoons chopped mint	*2 tablespoons chopped mint*
juice of 1 grapefruit	*juice of 1 grapefruit*
salt	*salt*
freshly ground black pepper	*freshly ground black pepper*
75 g/3 oz mung sprouts	*1 1/2 cups mung sprouts*
75 g/3 oz lentil sprouts	*1 1/2 cups lentil sprouts*
100 g/4 oz tiny broccoli florets	*1 cup tiny broccoli flowerets*
2 large courgettes, coarsely grated	*2 large zucchini, coarsely grated*
1 large grapefruit, peeled and cut into segments	*1 large grapefruit, peeled and cut into segments*
mint sprigs, to garnish	*mint sprigs, to garnish*

1. Skin the cooked chicken. Remove the flesh in strips and place in a shallow dish.
2. Mix the chopped mint with the grapefruit juice and add salt and pepper to taste. Stir into the chicken, cover and chill for 20 to 30 minutes.
3. Toss the chicken lightly with the mung sprouts, lentil sprouts, broccoli florets, grated courgettes (zucchini) and grapefruit segments. Garnish with sprigs of mint. ·2·6·8·

Dressed Avocado

Metric/Imperial	American
3 firm ripe avocados, peeled, stoned and cubed	*3 firm ripe avocados, peeled, pitted and cubed*
1 large cooked potato, diced	*1 large cooked potato, diced*
1 onion, sliced	*1 onion, sliced*
chervil sprigs, to garnish	*chervil sprigs, to garnish*
Vinaigrette Dressing:	Vinaigrette Dressing:
3 tablespoons olive oil	*3 tablespoons olive oil*
1 small clove garlic, peeled and crushed	*1 small clove garlic, peeled and crushed*

2 tablespoons white wine
   vinegar
2 tablespoons orange juice
1 tablespoon lemon juice
freshly ground black pepper

2 tablespoons white wine
   vinegar
2 tablespoons orange juice
1 tablespoon lemon juice
freshly ground black pepper

1. Just before serving place the avocados in a salad bowl with the diced potato and onion rings. Mix gently.
2. Combine all the dressing ingredients, whisk with a fork to blend thoroughly and pour over the salad. Make sure the avocado is well coated in dressing to avoid discoloration. To avoid mashing the avocado, fork gently through the salad and garnish with the chervil. ·2·7·

Sprouting chicken salad

Spicy Tomatoes

Metric/Imperial

4 large ripe tomatoes
3 spring onions, including
   some green tops, finely
   chopped
1 tablespoon lime juice
3/4 teaspoon grated fresh
   root ginger
salt
freshly ground black pepper

American

4 large ripe tomatoes
3 scallions, including some
   green tops, finely chopped
1 tablespoon lime juice
3/4 teaspoon grated fresh
   root ginger
salt
freshly ground black pepper

1. Cut the tomatoes crossways into thin slices and arrange in overlapping circles on a platter.
2. Sprinkle with the spring onion (scallion), lime juice, ginger and salt and pepper to taste. ·2·8·

Hot Cheese and Anchovy Bread

Metric/Imperial	American
1 loaf crusty Italian bread	1 loaf crusty Italian bread
4 tablespoons olive oil	1/4 cup olive oil
75 g/3 oz butter, softened	1/3 cup butter, softened
1 clove garlic, peeled and crushed	1 clove garlic, peeled and crushed
1 small can anchovy fillets, drained	1 small can anchovy fillets, drained
100 g/4 oz mozzarella or provolone cheese, shredded	1/4 lb mozzarella or provolone cheese, shredded
2 tablespoons capers, drained and chopped	2 tablespoons capers, drained and chopped

1. Slice the loaf in half lengthways. Combine the olive oil, butter, garlic and anchovies in a small bowl, mashing to a smooth paste.
2. Spread on both halves of the bread, and sprinkle one half with the cheese and capers. Press the halves together and wrap tightly in foil.
3. Heat in a preheated oven (240°C/475°F), Gas Mark 9 for 10 minutes. ·2·

Strawberry and Cointreau Crush

Metric/Imperial	American
250 g/8 oz strawberries, hulled	1/2 lb strawberries, hulled
2 tablespoons caster sugar	2 tablespoons sugar
1-2 tablespoons Cointreau	1-2 tablespoons Cointreau
250 ml/8 fl oz double or whipping cream	1 cup heavy or whipping cream

1. Reserve 4 to 6 small strawberries for decoration. Roughly crush the remainder with the sugar.

2. Place the Cointreau and cream in a bowl and whip until stiff. Fold the strawberry mixture into the cream.
3. Spoon into individual glass dishes. Slice the reserved strawberries and use to decorate. Chill until required.

C · O · U · N · T · D · O · W · N

To serve at 1.00 pm:

12.00: Chill the white wine. Prepare and blend all the ingredients for the Gazpacho. Add the water and chill. Prepare the garnishes, and refrigerate.

12.10: If serving the wine cup, marinate the orange and lemon slices in the brandy. Prepare the Strawberry and Cointreau Crush.

12.20: Prepare the cooked chicken and marinate in the grapefruit juice mixture for 20 to 30 minutes.

12.25: Prepare the Spicy Tomatoes.

12.30: Preheat the oven. Make up the Hot Cheese and Anchovy Bread, wrap tightly in foil.

About 12.40: Prepare the salad ingredients for the Sprouting Chicken Salad and mix with the chicken.

12.50: Heat the bread in the oven. Prepare the dressing for the avocados; but only prepare the avocados just before serving.

1.00: Add the chilled wine and lemonade or soda to the brandy and fruit and serve the White Wine Cup as your guests arrive. Follow with the Gazpacho.

F · R · E · E · Z · E · R · N · O · T · E · S

Only the Hot Cheese and Anchovy Bread will freeze. Savoury breads are a perfect standby to have in your freezer. Buy several Italian loaves or French sticks and prepare a variety of savoury fillings (see page 11). Wrap each loaf tightly in foil and freeze. To serve, take the bread straight from the freezer and bake in a preheated oven (190°C/375°F), Gas Mark 5 for about 30 minutes.

Cook's Tip:

Cover 1 or 2 peeled garlic bulbs with olive oil in a screw top jar. Use the oil in dressings.

△ M·E·N·U △

· 4 ·

Formal Dinner for 4

Prawn Pâté

·

Beef Steaks with Orange
Sautéed Mushrooms
Stir-fried Spiced Courgettes

·

Coffee and Chestnut Parfait
Florentine Biscuits

This speedy and simple yet elegant dinner party menu can be prepared in 1 hour – perfect for those last-minute important occasions, such as entertaining a business associate or when a young bride has to entertain her new in-laws at short notice!

Different Vegetable Accompaniments

Break away from tradition by serving Stir-fried Spiced Courgettes as the main course accompaniment. Courgettes tend to be rather bland if just boiled but here they are stir-fried with a little ginger, coriander and soy sauce; the perfect complement to grilled (broiled) steak. If you can't find fresh coriander just double up on the garlic.

Choosing the Wine

Serve a dry white wine with the Prawn Pâté, maybe a Chablis. Chill white wine for at least 2 hours in the refrigerator before serving. Serve a red wine with more body, such as a Chianti or Mâcon, with the steak. Open the bottle of red wine at least 2 hours before serving so that the wine has plenty of time to breathe.

Prawn Pâté

Metric/Imperial	American
125 g/4 oz butter	½ cup butter
1 clove garlic, peeled and crushed	1 clove garlic, peeled and crushed
1 teaspoon coriander seeds, crushed	1 teaspoon coriander seeds, crushed
125 g/4 oz peeled prawns	⅔ cup shelled shrimp
3 tablespoons double or whipping cream	3 tablespoons heavy or whipping cream
salt	salt
cayenne pepper	cayenne pepper
To Garnish:	To Garnish:
unpeeled prawns	unshelled shrimp
sprigs of parsley	sprigs of parsley
lemon wedges	lemon wedges

1. Melt the butter in a heavy frying pan (skillet) over a low heat and sauté the garlic and coriander for 2 to 3 minutes.
2. Add the prawns (shrimp) and turn to coat with the butter.
3. Transfer the contents of the pan to a blender or food processor and blend until smooth. Add the cream and blend again briefly. Add salt and cayenne pepper to taste.
4. Spoon the pâté into individual pots, level the surface with a round-bladed knife and chill well. Just before serving, garnish the pâté with prawns (shrimp) and parsley, then serve with wholemeal (wholewheat) toast and lemon wedges. ·1·6·10·

Rescue Tactic:
If the prawns lack flavour, add 1 to 2 teaspoons anchovy essence.

Beef Steaks with Orange

Metric/Imperial	American
4 thin rump steaks	4 thin top round steaks
4 tablespoons white wine	4 tablespoons white wine
2 tablespoons olive oil	2 tablespoons olive oil
juice of 1 orange	juice of 1 orange
salt	salt
freshly ground black pepper	freshly ground black pepper
1 clove garlic, peeled and crushed	1 clove garlic, peeled and crushed
orange twists, to garnish	orange twists, to garnish

1. Beat the steaks with a rolling pin or mallet to tenderize. Place in a large shallow bowl. Mix all the other ingredients together, except the orange twists, and pour over the meat in the bowl. Leave to marinate in a cool place for as long as possible.
2. Drain off the marinade. Grill (broil) the steaks under a preheated hot grill (broiler) for 10 minutes.
3. Arrange on a warm serving plate, garnish with orange twists and serve. ·2·10·

Sautéed Mushrooms

Metric/Imperial	American
750 g/1½ lb mushrooms	1½ lb mushrooms
7 tablespoons oil	7 tablespoons oil
2 cloves garlic, peeled and crushed	2 cloves garlic, peeled and crushed
2 tablespoons chopped oregano (or any other fresh herb)	2 tablespoons chopped oregano (or any other fresh herb)
salt	salt
freshly ground black pepper	freshly ground black pepper
grated nutmeg	grated nutmeg

1. Wipe over the mushrooms with a damp cloth and trim the stalks, then slice.
2. Heat the oil in a frying pan (skillet) over a fairly high heat and sauté the mushrooms, a few at a time.
3. When all the mushrooms are browned return to the pan, reduce the heat and add the garlic, oregano, salt, pepper and grated nutmeg to taste.
4. Cook gently for about 2 minutes, stirring occasionally. ·3·11·14·

Stir-fried Spiced Courgettes

Metric/Imperial	American
750 g/1½ lb large courgettes, peeled and cut into 2.5 cm/1 inch cubes	1½ lb zucchini, peeled and cut into 1 inch cubes
salt	salt
3 tablespoons oil	3 tablespoons oil
3 spring onions, sliced	3 scallions, sliced
1 clove garlic, peeled and chopped	1 clove garlic, peeled and chopped
1 tablespoon chopped fresh root ginger	1 tablespoon chopped fresh root ginger
1 tablespoon chopped coriander	1 tablespoon chopped coriander
1 teaspoon light soy sauce	1 teaspoon light soy sauce
2 tablespoons chicken stock or hot water	2 tablespoons chicken stock or hot water

1. Sprinkle the courgettes (zucchini) with salt and leave to drain for 30 minutes. Pat dry with absorbent kitchen paper.
2. Heat a wok or deep frying pan (skillet), add the oil and heat again. Stir-fry the spring onions (scallions), garlic, ginger and coriander over high heat for 1 to 2 minutes.
3. Add the courgettes and stir-fry for a further 2 minutes, then cover and simmer for another 2 minutes over a gentle heat. Add the soy sauce and stock, and stir-fry for 30 seconds. Turn the courgettes into a warm serving dish and serve. ·11·12·

Variation:

If courgettes are unobtainable use cucumber in the same way. Fresh coriander is an acquired taste. Use a mixture of chopped fresh herbs as an alternative and omit the ginger. Try parsley, chives and thyme or parsley and sage.

Coffee and chestnut parfait

Coffee and Chestnut Parfait

Metric/Imperial	American
1 × 425 g/15 oz can unsweetened chestnut purée	1 × 15 oz can unsweetened chestnut purée
2 teaspoons instant coffee powder	2 teaspoons instant coffee powder
4 tablespoons boiling water	4 tablespoons boiling water
50 g/2 oz caster sugar	1/4 cup sugar
150 ml/1/4 pint double or whipping cream	2/3 cup heavy or whipping cream
chopped pistachio nuts, to decorate	chopped pistachio nuts, to decorate
Florentine biscuits, to serve	Florentine biscuits, to serve

1. Mash the chestnut purée until softened.
2. Dissolve the instant coffee in the boiling water and beat into the chestnut purée, together with the sugar.
3. Whip the cream until soft peaks form, then fold lightly but thoroughly into the chestnut mixture.
4. Spoon the mixture into four tall stemmed glasses and chill.
5. Sprinkle with chopped pistachio and serve with Florentine Biscuits. ·1·

Florentine Biscuits

Metric/Imperial	American
50 g/2 oz soft margarine	1/4 cup soft margarine
50 g/2 oz caster sugar	1/4 cup sugar
50 g/2 oz chopped mixed nuts	1/2 cup chopped mixed nuts
1 1/2 tablespoons chopped raisins	1 1/2 tablespoons chopped raisins
1 1/2 tablespoons chopped glacé cherries	1 1/2 tablespoons chopped glacé cherries
1 1/2 tablespoons chopped mixed peel	1 1/2 tablespoons chopped mixed peel
1 tablespoon plain flour	1 tablespoon all-purpose flour
50 g/2 oz cooking chocolate	2 squares (1 oz each) cooking chocolate

1. Line two baking sheets with non-stick (parchment) paper. Melt the margarine in a pan over a gentle heat. Add the sugar, dissolve, then boil for 1 minute. Remove from the heat and stir in all ingredients, except chocolate.
2. Drop small teaspoons of the mixture on to the prepared baking sheets, about 5 cm (2 inches) apart. Cook in a preheated oven (180°C/350°F), Gas Mark 4 for 10 to 15 minutes. Cool on a wire rack.
3. Coat the undersides of the Florentines with melted chocolate, then cool. Makes about 6 to 8.

C · O · U · N · T · D · O · W · N

To serve at 8 pm:

6.00: Open the red wine.

7.00: Chill the white wine. Combine the ingredients for the steak marinade, marinate the steaks. Dice the courgettes, sprinkle with salt and leave to stand for 30 minutes.

7.10: Prepare the Prawn Pâté mixture and spoon into individual serving pots. Garnish, cover and refrigerate.

7.20: Prepare the Coffee and Chestnut Parfait, sprinkle with chopped pistachios, cover and refrigerate.

7.30: Preheat the oven for the oven chips, if using, following the packet instructions.

7.35: Preheat the grill. Slice and sauté the mushrooms. Transfer to a warm serving dish, cover and keep warm.

7.45: Place the oven chips in the oven to cook – about 350 g/12 oz. Drain the steaks and grill (broil) them for 5 minutes on each side. While grilling the steaks, stir-fry the courgettes.

7.55: Toast some bread to serve with the Prawn Pâté.

8.00: Keep the steaks and courgettes warm while serving the Prawn Pâté with toast.

△ M·E·N·U △

· 5 ·

Casual Brunch Buffet for 8

Yogurt Wholemeal Scones

·

Creamed Haddock
Eggs Provençal
Chicken and Peanut Pan Sandwich

·

Compote of Summer Fruits

This casual brunch menu is perfect for weekend entertaining, possibly in the sun. Although served at an unusual time – in the morning – this meal takes remarkably little time to put together.

Table Dressing
Create a summery feel by using a bright orange or yellow cloth with matching napkins. Pile up the crockery on the table (ordinary breakfast ware is fine). Arrange the cooked dishes buffet-style so your guests can help themselves. Serving this way is one of the easiest forms of catering for a larger number of people.

What to Drink
Fresh orange juice is the perfect drink to serve at any brunch. For special occasions serve Bucks Fizz – mix equal quantities of a sparkling dry white wine, such as Asti Spumante, with fresh orange juice. Your non-drinking friends may prefer to try this Breakfast Punch. Peel and stone (pit) 3 ripe peaches, and peel and core 3 ripe pears. Place the fruit in a blender or food processor with the juice of 1 lemon and purée until smooth. Add 1 litre/1¾ pints (4 cups) apple juice, and serve.

Yogurt Wholemeal Scones

Metric/Imperial
250 g/8 oz wholemeal flour
½ teaspoon salt
1½ teaspoons baking
    powder
25 g/1 oz vegetable
    margarine
150 ml/5 fl oz natural
    yogurt
To Serve:
honey
full-fat soft cheese

American
2 cups wholemeal flour
½ teaspoon salt
1½ teaspoons baking soda
2 tablespoons vegetable
    margarine
⅔ cup unflavored yogurt
To Serve:
honey
full-fat curd cheese

1. Put the flour, salt and baking powder (soda) in a bowl and stir well to mix. Rub (cut) in the margarine, then stir in the yogurt and mix to a soft dough.

2. Turn out onto a lightly floured surface and knead lightly for 30 seconds. Roll out to 2 cm/¾ inch thickness, cut out 10 rounds with a 5 cm/2 inch cutter and place on a greased baking sheet.

3. Bake in a preheated oven (200°C/400°F), Gas Mark 6 for 12 minutes. Transfer to a wire rack and leave to cool. Serve with honey and soft (curd) cheese.

Creamed Haddock

Metric/Imperial
250 g/8 oz smoked haddock
    fillet, cut into cubes

American
½ lb smoked haddock
    fillet, cut into cubes

plain flour	all-purpose flour
salt	salt
freshly ground black pepper	freshly ground black pepper
50 g/2 oz butter	1/4 cup butter
1 lean back bacon rasher, rind removed, finely chopped	1 slice lean bacon, rind removed, finely chopped
75 g/3 oz button mushrooms, sliced	3/4 cup sliced button mushrooms
150 ml/1/4 pint single cream	2/3 cup light cream
finely chopped parsley, to garnish	finely chopped parsley, to garnish

1. Coat the haddock lightly in flour seasoned with salt and pepper. Melt 25 g/1 oz (2 tablespoons) of the butter in a shallow frying pan (skillet) and gently cook the fish for about 2 minutes, turning once.
2. Meanwhile, melt the remaining butter in another pan and sauté the bacon and mushrooms until the mushrooms are just tender. Drain.
3. Stir the cream into the fish and simmer gently for 2 minutes. Stir the bacon and mushrooms into the fish mixture. Taste and adjust the seasoning.
4. Spoon into a warm serving dish and sprinkle with chopped parsley.

Eggs Provençal

Metric/Imperial	American
4 tablespoons oil	4 tablespoons oil
250 g/8 oz onions, sliced	1/2 lb onions, sliced
2 cloves garlic	2 cloves garlic
250 g/8 oz courgettes, sliced	1 1/2 cups sliced zucchini
2 tablespoons parsley	2 tablespoons parsley
1 × 400 g/14 oz can tomatoes	1 × 1 lb can tomatoes
	salt
	freshly ground black pepper

Chicken and peanut pan sandwich served with fried banana.

salt	8 eggs
freshly ground black pepper	
8 eggs	

1. Heat the oil in a frying pan (skillet) and sauté the onions and garlic for 3 to 4 minutes. Add the courgettes (zucchini) and fry for a further 3 to 4 minutes. Discard the garlic.
2. Stir in the basil and parsley, tomatoes, salt and pepper to taste. Spoon the mixture into a large ovenproof dish.
3. Make eight hollows in the mixture and break an egg in each. Cook in a preheated oven (190°C/375°F), Gas Mark 5 for 10 to 15 minutes or until the eggs are set.

Chicken and Peanut Pan Sandwich

Metric/Imperial	American
8 medium thick slices of bread	8 medium thick slices of bread
3 tablespoons peanut butter	3 tablespoons peanut butter
250 g/8 oz cooked sliced chicken	generous 1 cup cooked sliced chicken
4 eggs	4 eggs
125 ml/4 fl oz milk	1/2 cup milk
salt	salt
freshly ground black pepper	freshly ground black pepper
2 bananas, peeled	2 bananas, peeled
175 g/6 oz butter	3/4 cup butter
sprigs of watercress, to garnish	sprigs of watercress, to garnish

1. Spread all the bread with the peanut butter and make four thick sandwiches with the sliced chicken. Press down well.
2. Beat eggs, milk and salt and pepper together. Pour a quarter of the mixture into a shallow dish. Dip one side of one sandwich in the mixture, turn

over and leave until remaining egg mixture is absorbed. Repeat with remaining egg mixture and sandwiches.

3. Cut the bananas in half lengthways.

4. Melt 75 g/3 oz (6 tablespoons) of the butter in a frying pan (skillet) and cook two sandwiches and half the banana pieces until golden brown, turning once. Drain and keep warm while frying the remaining sandwiches. Garnish the Chicken and Peanut Pan sandwiches with sprigs of watercress.

Variation:

Cheese and Ham Pan Sandwich:

Spread the bread with mustard and make sandwiches with sliced Cheddar cheese and ham. Coat in the egg mixture and fry as above. Serve with sautéed pineapple slices instead of banana.

Apple and Pickle Pan Sandwich:

Spread wholemeal bread with sweet pickle. Make sandwiches with thinly sliced apple and Gouda cheese. Coat in the egg mixture and fry as above. Serve with extra slices of apple.

Compote of Summer Fruits

Metric/Imperial	American
300 ml/1/2 pint water	1 1/4 cups water
150 g/6 oz granulated sugar	3/4 cup sugar
2 sticks of cinnamon	2 sticks of cinnamon
thinly pared rind of 1 orange	thinly pared rind of 1 orange
300 ml/1/2 pint red wine or orange juice	1 1/4 cups red wine or orange juice
250 g/8 oz raspberries	2 cups raspberries
500 g/1 lb strawberries	4 cups strawberries
250 g/8 oz redcurrants	2 cups red currants
250 g/8 oz blackcurrants	2 cups black currants

1. Put the water, sugar, cinnamon sticks and orange rind into a saucepan and gradually bring to the boil, stirring to dissolve the sugar.

2. Stir in the wine, boil for 2 minutes, remove from the heat and leave to cool.

3. Prepare the soft fruits: hull the strawberries, string the currants. Put the fruit into a serving dish. Spoon over the cooled syrup.

4. Cover and refrigerate. Serve chilled. ·12·

C · O · U · N · T · D · O · W · N

On the day:

Set the table. Prepare the fruit for the punch, if making.

To serve at 11 am:

10.00: Chill fruit juices and wine, if using. Make the sugar syrup for the Compote of Summer Fruits and leave to cool. Prepare the fruit and place in the serving bowl.

10.10: Prepare and fry the vegetable mixture for the Eggs Provençal. Spoon into the serving dish, shape the hollows but do not add the eggs.

10.15: Preheat the oven.

10.20: Pour the cooled syrup over the fruit, cover and refrigerate. Prepare the Chicken and Peanut Pan Sandwiches but do not cook. Set aside.

10.30: Prepare the Yogurt Wholemeal Scones, shape and bake.

10.40: Break the eggs into the vegetable mixture and bake at the bottom of the oven. Fry the pan sandwiches together with the banana garnish.

10.45: While the pan sandwiches are frying, prepare the Creamed Haddock.

10.55: Finish the punch. Place the Creamed Haddock and pan sandwiches on serving dishes and garnish.

11.00: Take the dishes and fruit juice etc to the table. Make up the Bucks Fizz as required.

F · R · E · E · Z · E · R · N · O · T · E · S

Only the Yogurt Wholemeal Scones will freeze. Cool, pack and freeze at the end of stage 3. Thaw at room temperature for 2 to 3 hours. Refresh at (200°C/400°F), Gas Mark 6 for 10 minutes.

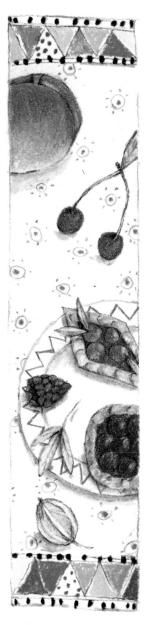

△ M · E · N · U △

· 6 ·

Italian Supper for 8

Antipasto

·

Risotto Marinara
Italian Salad

·

Zabaglione
Almond and Ginger Snaps
Biscuit Rings

This colourful menu, with an authentic Italian flavour, takes only 30 minutes to prepare. Other than the fresh salad ingredients, it is put together using mostly canned ingredients; perfect for spur-of-the-moment suppers, as long as you have a well-stocked store cupboard.

For Best Effect

The ingredients for the Antipasto should be attractively arranged on an extremely large platter. If you don't have one, you could use a large, well-cleaned tray. You can vary the ingredients — left-over ham, hard-boiled (hard-cooked) eggs, canned haricot (navy) beans can all be used in place of the more extravagant ingredients used here.

The Sweet Finale

Prepare the Zabaglione after you have cleared away the main course. Complete the meal with a selection of Italian cheeses served with grapes, peaches or other fresh fruit in season, along with a good Italian coffee — on the strong side.

Serve a good-quality Chianti throughout the meal.

Antipasto

Metric/Imperial	American
1 × 50 g/1¾ oz can anchovies	1 × 2 oz can anchovies
1 × 198 g/7 oz can tuna	1 × 7 oz can tuna
250 g/8 oz peeled prawns	1½ cups shelled shrimp
1 × 120 g/4¼ oz can sardines	1 × 4¼ oz can sardines
250 g/8 oz Mortadella sausage, sliced	½ lb Mortadella sausage, sliced
250 g/8 oz salami, thinly sliced	½ lb salami, thinly sliced
4 hard-boiled eggs, quartered	4 hard-cooked eggs, quartered
½ cucumber, sliced	½ cucumber, sliced
4 tomatoes, quartered	4 tomatoes, quartered
1 × 400 g/14 oz can artichoke hearts	1 × 16 oz can artichoke hearts
cos lettuce	bibb lettuce
olive oil	olive oil
wine vinegar	wine vinegar

1. Attractively arrange these foods, or a selection of them, on a large platter.
2. Pour over a little oil and vinegar and serve immediately. ·8·

Risotto Marinara

Metric/Imperial	American
4 tablespoons olive oil	4 tablespoons olive oil
2 cloves garlic, peeled and crushed	2 cloves garlic, peeled and crushed
250 g/8 oz long-grain rice	1 cup long-grain rice
2 × 250 g/9 oz cans baby clams, drained	2 × 9 oz cans baby clams, drained
2 × 250 g/9 oz cans mussels in brine, drained	2 × 9 oz cans mussels in brine, drained
600 ml/1 pint fish or chicken stock	2½ cups fish or chicken stock
2 tablespoons coarsely chopped parsley	2 tablespoons coarsely chopped parsley
grissini (bread sticks)	grissini (bread sticks)

1. Heat the oil in a saucepan and sauté the garlic for 1 minute.
2. Stir in the rice and sauté until the rice is golden brown, stirring all the time to prevent burning.
3. Stir in the clams, mussels and stock. Bring to the boil, then lower heat.
4. Cover and simmer for 15 minutes or until the rice is tender and the liquid absorbed.
5. Fluff up the mixture with a fork and stir in the parsley. Serve immediately with grissini.

Cook's Tip:
If time allows, drain the clams and mussels and soak in milk for 20 minutes to remove excess salt.

Italian Salad

Metric/Imperial	American
1 curly endive, separated into leaves	1 head chicory, separated into leaves
1 head chicory, sliced into rings	1 head endive, sliced into rings
1 bulb fennel, sliced into rings	1 bulb fennel, sliced into rings
1 head radicchio, separated into leaves	1 head red chicory, separated into leaves
8 radishes, sliced if large	8 radishes, sliced if large
4 tablespoons Vinaigrette Dressing (page 14/15)	¼ cup Vinaigrette Dressing (page 14/15)
salt	salt
freshly ground black pepper	freshly ground black pepper

1. Put all the salad ingredients in a salad bowl. Add the dressing and toss well to ensure that ingredients are well coated.
2. Taste and adjust the seasoning. ·2·7·8·

Zabaglione; Almond and ginger snaps

Zabaglione

Metric/Imperial	American
6 egg yolks	6 egg yolks
125 g/4 oz caster sugar	1/2 cup superfine sugar
10 tablespoons Marsala	10 tablespoons Marsala

1. Whisk the yolks and sugar in a bowl until creamy and white. Add the Marsala.
2. Stand the bowl over a pan of simmering water (the bowl should not touch the water) and whisk the mixture until it thickens and becomes spongy.
3. Pour into four wine glasses and serve accompanied by Almond and Ginger Snaps.

Almond and Ginger Snaps

Metric/Imperial	American
125 g/4 oz flaked almonds	1 cup slivered almonds
25 g/1 oz preserved ginger, finely diced	2 tablespoons finely diced preserved ginger
20 g/3/4 oz plain flour	3 tablespoons all-purpose flour
140 g/4 1/2 oz sugar	generous 1/2 cup sugar
25 g/1 oz butter, melted	2 tablespoons melted butter
2 egg whites	2 egg whites
15 g/1/2 oz flaked almonds, to decorate	1 tablespoon slivered almonds, to decorate

1. Mix the almonds, ginger, flour and sugar in a bowl. Beat in the melted butter, then the egg whites. (It does not matter if the almonds break up.)
2. Line two large baking sheets with non-stick silicone paper. Arrange teaspoons of the mixture on the paper, about 12 to a sheet. Flatten each spoonful with the back of a fork dipped in water. Decorate each snap with flaked almonds. Bake in a preheated oven (200°C/400°F), Gas Mark 6 for 12 minutes.
3. Remove the baking sheet from the oven and cool the snaps for about 30 seconds. Lift the snaps one by one and shape over a rolling pin until cool.

Biscuit Rings

Biscuit Rings

Metric/Imperial
450 g/1 lb fine maize flour
50 g/2 oz plain flour
250 g/9 oz butter, cut into
  small pieces
225 g/8 oz sugar
3 eggs, beaten

American
4 cups fine maize flour
½ cup all-purpose flour
1 cup plus 2 tablespoons
  butter, cut into small
  pieces
1¼ cups sugar

finely grated rind of
  ½ lemon

3 eggs, beaten
finely grated rind of
  ½ lemon

1. Mix the two flours together in a bowl and rub in the butter, using the fingertips. The mixture should resemble fine breadcrumbs. Add the sugar, eggs and lemon rind, then knead well together until smooth using a little extra flour if necessary.
2. Put the mixture into a piping (pastry) bag, fitted with a 1 cm/½ inch plain nozzle, and pipe small rings, spaced well apart onto a baking (cookie) sheet. Chill for 10 to 15 minutes.
3. Bake in a preheated oven (180°C/350°F) Gas Mark 4 for 20 minutes or until golden. Leave on the sheets for 5 minutes, then transfer to a wire rack and cool completely.

C · O · U · N · T · D · O · W · N
On the day:
Make and bake the Almond and Ginger Snaps and the Biscuit Rings. Store in airtight containers.
To serve at 8 pm:
6.00: Open the red wine.
7.30: Prepare the vegetables for the Italian Salad and place in a salad bowl. Make up the dressing.
7.40: Prepare the Risotto Marinara.
7.50: Assemble the ingredients for the Zabaglione and set aside. Prepare the Antipasto and arrange on a large platter.
7.55: Toss the Italian Salad in the dressing. Fork through the risotto.
8.00: Serve the Antipasto.
Between courses: Make the Zabaglione.

Cook's Tip:
If there are any left-over Almond and Ginger Snaps, or Biscuit Rings, store them in an airtight container. They will keep for a week to ten days.

F · R · E · E · Z · E · R · N · O · T · E · S
None of the dishes is suitable for freezing.

△ M · E · N · U △

· 7 ·

Vegetarian Supper for 4

Spaghetti with Buttered Mushrooms
·

Walnut and Cheese Burgers
White Bean Salad
Melon Salad
·

Apricot Toasts

This varied meatless menu is the perfect answer for when vegetarian friends are coming to dinner. Alternatively, use it to introduce your family to meatless meals.

For Health

For once medical authorities are all of the same opinion: we should reduce the amount of animal fats and proteins we consume, and obtain more of our protein from vegetable sources. Make a habit of serving one vegetarian meal a week. If liked, these can be increased in frequency as your family adjusts to the idea of some meals without meat. Always make a point of serving wholemeal bread and use low-fat alternatives wherever possible – skimmed milk, low-fat cheeses, etc.

Red or White Wine?

When eating meatless meals, the choice of red or white wine is yours. Either a young red Bordeaux, a crisp Frascati or a dry white Soave would complement this meal. Open the red two hours before serving to allow the wine to breathe and white wine should be chilled an hour or so before your meal.

Spaghetti with Buttered Mushrooms

Metric/Imperial	American
250 g/8 oz wholemeal spaghetti	1/2 lb wholewheat spaghetti
50 g/2 oz butter	1/4 cup butter
250 g/8 oz mushrooms, thinly sliced	2 cups thinly sliced mushrooms
pinch of grated nutmeg	pinch of grated nutmeg
125 g/4 oz Cheddar cheese, grated	1 cup grated Cheddar cheese
4 tablespoons grated Parmesan cheese	4 tablespoons grated Parmesan cheese
salt	salt
freshly ground black pepper	freshly ground black pepper

1. Cook the spaghetti in a large saucepan of boiling salted water for about 10 minutes until just tender. Drain in a colander, pour over hot water, then drain again thoroughly.
2. Melt the butter in the pan and sauté the mushrooms for a few minutes until soft.
3. Return the spaghetti to the pan, with the nutmeg, cheeses and salt and pepper to taste. Mix well and serve immediately. ·11·

Walnut and Cheese Burgers

Metric/Imperial	American
175 g/6 oz shelled walnuts	1 1/2 cups shelled walnuts
50 g/2 oz wholemeal bread, cubed	2 large slices wholewheat bread, cubed
125 g/4 oz Cheddar cheese, grated	1 cup grated Cheddar cheese
1 onion, grated	1 onion, grated
salt	salt
freshly ground black pepper	freshly ground black pepper
	1 egg
1 egg	1 tablespoon tomato paste
1 tablespoon tomato purée	oil, for shallow frying
oil, for shallow frying	

1. Put 125 g/4 oz (1 cup) of the nuts in a blender or food processor. Add the bread and grind coarsely.
2. Transfer to a bowl, add the cheese, onion and salt and pepper to taste, and stir well. Beat the egg with the tomato purée (paste). Add the egg and tomato purée mixture to the nut mixture and stir together until well combined.
3. Divide the mixture into four on a slightly floured surface. Shape into burgers, about 8 cm/3 1/2 inches in diameter and 1 cm/1/2 inch thick. Chop the reserved walnuts and press into both sides of the burgers.
4. Heat a little oil in a frying pan (skillet) and fry the burgers for about 5 minutes until browned on both sides, turning once. Alternatively, place the burgers on a lightly greased baking sheet and bake in a preheated oven (200°C/400°F), Gas Mark 6 for 20 minutes until browned.
5. Serve hot or cold.

White Bean Salad

Metric/Imperial	American
500 g/1 lb canned white beans, drained weight (mixture of haricot, butter beans, and black-eye peas)	1 lb canned white beans, drained weight (mixture of navy, lima beans, and black-eye peas)
1 onion, chopped	1 onion, chopped
3 tablespoons olive oil	3 tablespoons olive oil
grated rind and juice of 1 small lemon	grated rind and juice of 1 small lemon
1 tablespoon capers	1 tablespoon capers
2 gherkins, sliced	2 gherkins, sliced
2 tablespoons chopped parsley	2 tablespoons chopped parsley
salt	salt
	freshly ground black pepper

freshly ground black pepper
2 hard-boiled eggs, cut into
   wedges
8 black olives

2 hard-cooked eggs, cut into
   wedges
8 ripe olives

1. Rinse the beans and drain. Mix with the onion. Stir well.

2. To make the dressing, mix together the oil, lemon rind and juice, capers, gherkins, parsley, and salt and pepper to taste. Pour half the dressing over the beans. Cover and leave to marinate in the refrigerator for at least 30 minutes or preferably overnight.

3. Spoon the beans into a serving dish and arrange the hard-boiled (hard-cooked) eggs and olives on the top. Add the remaining dressing and serve.

Spaghetti with buttered mushrooms

Melon Salad

Metric/Imperial	American
2 ripe honeydew or ogen melons, halved, seeded and peeled	2 ripe honeydew or ogen melons, halved, seeded and peeled
1 small red pepper, cored, seeded and sliced	1 small red pepper, cored, seeded and sliced
2 tablespoons lemon juice	2 tablespoons lemon juice
1 tablespoon vegetable oil	1 tablespoon vegetable oil
1 teaspoon ground ginger	1 teaspoon ground ginger
fresh salad vegetables, e.g. lettuce, cucumber, celery, to garnish	fresh salad vegetables, e.g. lettuce, cucumber, celery, to garnish

1. Cut the melon flesh into 2.5 cm/1 inch cubes and put in a bowl with the red pepper.
2. Combine the lemon juice with the oil and pour over the melon.
3. Sprinkle the ginger on top and fork through lightly to coat the melon with the dressing.
4. Arrange the salad vegetables in a serving dish and spoon in the melon salad. ·2·3·8·

Variation:
1 teaspoon peeled and grated fresh root ginger can be substituted for ground to give extra bite.

Apricot Toasts

Metric/Imperial	American
1 egg	*1 egg*
1 tablespoon milk	*1 tablespoon milk*
4 small slices fruit, malt or wholemeal bread, crusts removed	*4 small slices fruit, malt or wholewheat bread, crusts removed*
40 g/1½ oz butter	*3 tablespoons butter*
2 tablespoons caster sugar	*2 tablespoons superfine sugar*
½ teaspoon ground cinnamon	*½ teaspoon ground cinnamon*
1 × 410 g/14 oz can apricot halves, drained	*1 × 16 oz can apricot halves, drained*
To Decorate:	To Decorate:
a little whipped cream	*a little whipped cream*
1 tablespoon chopped pistachios or toasted almonds	*1 tablespoon chopped pistachios or toasted almonds*

1. Beat the egg and milk together. Dip the bread slices in the egg mixture until coated on both sides.
2. Melt the butter in a frying pan (skillet) and fry the slices of bread until crisp and golden on both sides. Drain on absorbent kitchen paper.
3. Mix together the sugar and cinnamon and sprinkle over the toasts. Top with apricot halves, a whirl of whipped cream and the chopped nuts.

·1·10·
Variation:
Vary the fruit by using canned or fresh currants and berry fruits – all high-fibre alternatives.

C · O · U · N · T · D · O · W · N

To serve at 8 pm:
6.00: Open the red wine, if using.
7.00: Chill the white wine, if using. Hard-boil (hard-cook) the eggs for the White Bean Salad. Rinse and drain the beans. Prepare the dressing and pour half of it over the beans. Leave to marinate.
7.10: Make, shape and coat the Walnut and Cheese Burgers.
7.20: Collect together the ingredients for the Apricot Toasts. Dip the bread into the egg mixture, cover and refrigerate.
7.25: Prepare the Melon Salad. Cover and re-frigerate.
7.35: Complete the White Bean Salad.
7.40: Fry the burgers. Drain and keep warm.
7.45: Cook the spaghetti. Meanwhile, prepare and sauté the mushrooms. Complete the Spaghetti with Buttered Mushrooms.
8.00: Garnish the dishes. Serve the spaghetti starter.
Between courses: Fry the Apricot Toasts, decorate and serve.

Cook's Tip:
To keep cooked spaghetti hot, cook in the usual way. Do not drain. Turn off the heat. Cover the pan with a tea towel and a lid. The spaghetti will keep hot for 10 to 12 minutes without over-cooking.

Rescue Tactic:
If the spaghetti is over-cooked make a sauce from the buttered mushrooms by adding 3 tablespoons of flour and 300 ml/½ pint milk. Place the spaghetti in a shallow heatproof dish. Pour over the sauce. Sprinkle with the Parmesan cheese and brown under a hot grill.

F · R · E · E · Z · E · R · N · O · T · E · S
None of the dishes is suitable for freezing.

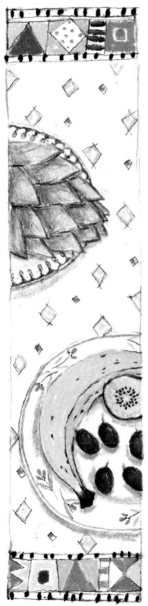

▲ M · E · N · U ▲

· 8 ·

Summer Lunch for 8

Parma Ham with Melon
·
Salad Niçoise
Red Cabbage with Soured Cream
or New Potato Salad
Leeks à la Grecque
·
Pineapple and Kirsch Roll

This light summer menu has a famous salad as its main dish. Salad Niçoise is a speciality of the resort town of Nice on the French Riviera. This is an earthy, strongly-flavoured, mixed salad with ingredients that can be varied according to the vegetables in season: lightly cooked cauliflower florets, raw carrot slivers and mangetouts (snow peas) are all possibilities, but olives, anchovies, hard-boiled (hard-cooked) eggs and tomatoes are essential to give the salad its typically Niçoise flavour.

Alternative Foods to Use

This is the perfect meal to choose for a spontaneous lunch party as it is full of possible alternatives depending upon the food stocked by your local delicatessen. It also illustrates how important it is to be flexible when shopping.

Smoked beef or salami can be used in place of the Parma ham, and fresh mangos can be used instead of the melon for the first course. Green beans or mushrooms can be substituted for the leeks in the Leeks à la Grecque.

The perfect wines for a salad meal are Orvieto, Frascati or a Mateus Rosé.

Parma Ham with Melon

Metric/Imperial	American
1 large ripe melon	*1 large ripe melon*
8 thin slices of Parma ham	*8 thin slices of Parma ham*

1. Chill the melon for 1 hour in the refrigerator.
2. Cut the melon into eight slices and remove the seeds. Place a portion of melon on each of eight individual serving plates.
3. Drape a slice of ham over each piece of melon. Serve immediately. ·2·3·4·

Variation:
Use 2 or 3 peeled and thickly sliced ripe mangos in place of the melon for an unusual and delicious alternative. Try a tablespoon of Vinaigrette Dressing (page 14/15) over each portion.

Parma ham with melon

Salad Niçoise

Metric/Imperial	American
1 large crisp lettuce	*1 large crisp lettuce*
2 heads radicchio	*2 heads radicchio*
250 g/8 oz firm tomatoes, quartered	*½ lb firm tomatoes, quartered*
175 g/6 oz stringless green beans, steamed and cooled	*6 oz stringless green beans, steamed and cooled*
4 hard-boiled eggs, quartered	*4 hard-cooked eggs, quartered*
1 × 90 g/3½ oz can tuna, drained and flaked	*1 × 3½ oz can tuna, drained and flaked*
8 anchovy fillets	*8 anchovy fillets*
50 g/2 oz black olives	*¼ cup ripe olives*
Dressing:	Dressing:
6 tablespoons olive oil	*6 tablespoons olive oil*
2 tablespoons vinegar	*2 tablespoons vinegar*
	1 teaspoon Dijon mustard

1 teaspoon French mustard
1 teaspoon lemon juice
salt
freshly ground black pepper
Aïoli:
2-3 cloves garlic, peeled
and crushed
½ teaspoon French
mustard
½ teaspoon salt
2 egg yolks
300 ml/½ pint olive oil

1 teaspoon lemon juice
salt
freshly ground black pepper
Aïoli:
2-3 cloves garlic, peeled
and crushed
½ teaspoon Dijon
mustard
½ teaspoon salt
2 egg yolks
1¼ cups olive oil

1. With the hands, break the lettuce and radicchio into even-sized pieces and arrange in a shallow salad bowl or on a large flat serving dish.
2. Arrange the tomatoes, green beans, eggs, tuna, anchovies and olives on top.
3. Thoroughly combine all the dressing ingredients.
4. Combine the garlic, mustard, salt and egg yolks in a blender or food processor until smooth. Put the olive oil in a small jug and add very gradually to the garlic mixture. Adjust the seasoning.
5. Pour a little of the vinaigrette dressing over the salad and hand the remainder separately with the aïoli.

Red Cabbage with Soured Cream

Metric/Imperial	American
1 small red cabbage, about 350 g/12 oz, shredded	1 small red cabbage, about ¾ lb, shredded
1 small mild onion, finely chopped	1 small mild onion, finely chopped
1 large cooking apple, peeled, cored and sliced	1 large tart apple, peeled, cored and sliced
1 teaspoon cumin seeds, crushed	1 teaspoon cumin seeds, crushed
1 teaspoon poppy seeds	1 teaspoon poppy seeds
Dressing:	Dressing:

150 ml/5 fl oz soured
cream
2 teaspoons French mustard
1 tablespoon wine vinegar
or lemon juice
2 teaspoons sugar
salt

⅔ cup sour cream
2 teaspoons French mustard
1 tablespoon wine vinegar
or lemon juice
2 teaspoons sugar
salt

1. Mix the cabbage, onion and apple together. Sprinkle with the cumin and poppy seeds.
2. Combine all the dressing ingredients and whisk with a fork to blend thoroughly. Pour over the salad and toss well. ·2·3·

Leeks à la Grecque

Metric/Imperial	American
8 young leeks	8 young leeks
125 g/4 oz button mushrooms	4 oz button mushrooms
1 tablespoon chopped fresh tarragon or 1 teaspoon dried	1 tablespoon chopped fresh tarragon or 1 teaspoon dried
4 teaspoons lemon juice	4 teaspoons lemon juice
1 clove garlic, peeled and crushed	1 clove garlic, peeled and crushed
1 tablespoon chopped parsley	1 tablespoon chopped parsley
1 tomato, skinned and seeded	1 tomato, peeled and seeded
pinch of dried thyme	pinch of dried thyme
salt	salt
freshly ground black pepper	freshly ground black pepper
1 bay leaf	1 bay leaf
4 tablespoons olive oil	¼ cup olive oil
250 ml/8 fl oz water	1 cup water

1. Trim the root ends of the leeks and remove any coarse outer leaves, as only the white part and a little of the green of leeks are used.
2. Slit the leeks right down one side and wash thoroughly under cold running water.

3. Place the leeks in a heavy saucepan large enough to take them whole.

4. Add the remaining ingredients. Cover the pan and bring to the boil. Reduce the heat and simmer for 8 to 10 minutes. Allow to cool, then chill.

New Potato Salad

Metric/Imperial	American
1 kg/2 lb new potatoes, scrubbed	*2 lb new potatoes, scrubbed*
salt	*salt*
Dressing:	*Dressing:*
2 tablespoons wine vinegar	*2 tablespoons wine vinegar*
1 tablespoon French mustard	*1 tablespoon Dijon mustard*
freshly ground black pepper	*freshly ground black pepper*
6 tablespoons olive oil	*6 tablespoons olive oil*
4 tablespoons chopped herbs	*4 tablespoons chopped herbs*

1. Cook the potatoes in a saucepan of boiling salted water until tender. Drain and dice.

2. To make the dressing, place all the ingredients in a screw-top jar and shake well.

3. Pour the dressing over the well-drained potatoes and leave to cool.

Pineapple and Kirsch Roll

Metric/Imperial	American
1 large ripe pineapple	*1 large ripe pineapple*
500 ml/16 fl oz double or whipping cream	*2 cups heavy or whipping cream*
125 g/4 oz macaroons	*1 cup macaroons*
2 tablespoons Kirsch	*2 tablespoons Kirsch*
angelica leaves, to decorate	*angelica leaves, to decorate*

1. Remove the green top from the pineapple and cut it in half lengthways, reserving the better half for decoration. Cut away the skin from the pineapple,

removing the 'eyes' with the point of a knife. Cut into slices, then cut each slice in half and blot dry with absorbent kitchen paper. Remove the core.

2. Lightly whip the cream and reserve one third. Stir the crushed macaroons into the remaining cream.

3. Sandwich the half-slices of pineapple together with the macaroon cream, and form into a half-roll on a flat serving plate.

4. Stir the Kirsch into the reserved cream and use to mask the pineapple completely. Mark the cream to look like pineapple skin.

5. To serve, decorate with angelica leaves and replace the green top. Chill until required.

C · O · U · N · T · D · O · W · N

On the day:
Start preparing the salad vegetables. Cover and refrigerate.

To serve at 1 pm:
11.45: Place the melon in the refrigerator.
12.00: Chill the wine. Clean the leeks, place in a saucepan with the remaining ingredients and cook. Prepare and steam the beans for the Salad Niçoise. Cook the eggs.
12.10: Prepare the dressing for the Salad Niçoise.
12.15: Cool, cover and chill the Leeks à la Grecque.
12.20: Prepare the Pineapple and Kirsch Roll.
12.40: Prepare the Red Cabbage with Soured Cream or the New Potato Salad. Combine with the dressing and toss well.
12.50: Arrange the Salad Niçoise on a serving platter and pour over a little dressing. Slice the melon and arrange on serving plates. Drape with Parma ham, then serve.

F · R · E · E · Z · E · R · N · O · T · E · S

The Pineapple and Kirsch Roll is best made and served on the day. It can be frozen but will give a slightly softer result. Open freeze at the end of stage 4. Wrap loosely. Thaw overnight in the refrigerator. Decorate as per recipe.

△ M · E · N · U △

· 9 ·

Simple Supper for 4

Chicken Liver Toasts
·
Cidered Fish Bake
Cheesy Potatoes
Avocado Sesame Salad
·
Scottish Honey Posset

This uncomplicated yet mouthwatering menu is perfect to feed family or friends; for less formal evenings omit the Avocado Sesame Salad.

Short Cuts and Variations

If time is short, serve baked potatoes in place of the Cheesy Potatoes. However, the Cheesy Potatoes are delicious and can be varied according to your taste. Use marjoram or oregano in place of the basil, and crumbled blue cheese instead of the Cheddar. For a less rich version, use natural (unflavored) yogurt instead of the cream. Add a few slices of ham or flaked tuna and you have a perfect supper dish. For an extra treat, serve a compote of in-season raspberries, strawberries and redcurrants with the Scottish Honey Posset.

Table Dressing

Even when entertaining friends on a casual basis it is necessary to make an effort with the table setting. Individual place mats with matching napkins are an attractive alternative to a tablecloth, and a flowering pot plant is a handsome substitute for fresh flowers.

For drinks, serve a dry cider with the main course.

Chicken Liver Toasts

Metric/Imperial	American
40 g/1½ oz butter, plus extra for shallow frying	3 tablespoons butter, plus extra for shallow frying
1 small shallot, finely chopped	1 small shallot, finely chopped
3-4 sage leaves	3-4 sage leaves
250 g/8 oz chicken livers, cleaned and finely chopped	½ lb chicken livers, cleaned and finely chopped
freshly ground black pepper	freshly ground black pepper
8 slices of bread, 5 mm/ ¼ inch thick, cut into triangles	8 slices of bread, ¼ inch thick, cut into triangles
1 teaspoon lemon juice	1 teaspoon lemon juice
1 tablespoon chopped parsley, to garnish	1 tablespoon chopped parsley, to garnish

1. Melt the 40 g/1½ oz (3 tablespoons) butter in a small saucepan and gently sauté the shallot and sage leaves for about 5 minutes until the shallots are golden and soft. Discard the sage leaves.
2. Add the chicken livers and pepper and cook gently, stirring frequently, for about 6 minutes or until the livers are no longer pink.
3. Meanwhile, fry the triangles of bread in the extra butter until crisp and golden on both sides. Do this over a moderate heat to avoid burning the butter. Drain on absorbent kitchen paper and keep warm while finishing liver mixture.
4. Stir the lemon juice into the liver mixture and adjust the seasoning. Spoon the liver mixture over the croûtes and sprinkle with parsley. ·1·8·12·

Rescue Tactic:
If the chicken livers are overcooked, cool slightly and then purée the contents of the pan in a blender or food processor. Spread on the hot bread. Garnish with parsley then cut the toasts into fingers or triangles and serve as an appetizer with pre-supper drinks.

Cidered Fish Bake

Metric/Imperial	American
75 g/3 oz butter	6 tablespoons butter
250 g/8 oz carrots, chopped	½ lb carrots, chopped
1 onion, chopped	1 onion, chopped
50 g/2 oz button mushrooms, sliced	½ cup sliced button mushrooms
4 halibut steaks	4 halibut steaks
salt	salt
freshly ground black pepper	freshly ground black pepper
250 ml/8 fl oz dry cider	1 cup hard cider
1 tablespoon cornflour	1 tablespoon cornstarch

1. Melt the butter in a saucepan and gently sauté the carrot and onion until soft. Add the mushrooms and cook for 1 minute.
2. Sprinkle the fish with salt and pepper and arrange in a shallow ovenproof dish.
3. Spoon over the vegetables and any remaining butter together with half the cider. Cover and cook in a preheated oven (180°C/350°F), Gas Mark 4 for about 30 minutes.
4. Remove the fish and place on a warm serving plate. Keep warm. Strain the cooking liquor and reserve the vegetables.
5. Blend the remaining cider with the cornflour (cornstarch) in a small saucepan to make a smooth paste. Stir in the cooking liquor and reserved vegetables and bring to the boil. Pour over the fish. ·2·11·

Cheesy Potatoes

Metric/Imperial	American
4 potatoes, peeled and thinly sliced	4 potatoes, peeled and thinly sliced
25 g/1 oz butter	2 tablespoons butter
1 onion, thinly sliced	1 onion, thinly sliced
1 clove garlic, peeled and crushed	1 clove garlic, peeled and crushed

¹/₂ teaspoon dried basil
salt
freshly ground black pepper
125 ml/4 fl oz milk
4 tablespoons single cream
50 g/2 oz Cheddar cheese,
grated

¹/₂ teaspoon dried basil
salt
freshly ground black pepper
¹/₂ cup milk
4 tablespoons light cream
¹/₂ cup grated Cheddar
cheese

1. Layer the sliced potatoes in a small buttered ovenproof dish with the onion, garlic, basil and salt and pepper to taste.
2. Mix together the milk and cream and spoon over the top. Dot with the remaining butter and sprinkle with the grated cheese.
3. Bake in a preheated oven (180°C/350°F), Gas Mark 4 for 40 to 50 minutes or until the potatoes are tender.

Note: If you are preparing this dish in advance, bake in the oven for only 20 minutes. Once cool, overwrap the dish and chill overnight. Heat through in a preheated oven (190°C/375°F), Gas Mark 5 for about 20 minutes. ·2·3·14·

Cidered fish bake

Avocado Sesame Salad

Metric/Imperial	American
2 large avocados	2 large avocados
juice of 1 small lemon	juice of 1 small lemon
2 grapefruit, peel and pith removed, divided into segments	2 grapefruit, peel and pith removed, divided into segments
1 tablespoon chopped mint	1 tablespoon chopped mint
1 small lettuce	1 small head lettuce
2 tablespoons sesame seeds	2 tablespoons sesame seeds
sprigs of mint, to garnish	sprigs of mint, to garnish

1. Peel the avocados, cut in half lengthways, then remove the stones (seeds). Slice the flesh, place in a bowl, then sprinkle with the lemon juice.
2. Fold the grapefruit and chopped mint into the avocado.
3. Arrange the lettuce leaves in individual serving bowls. Divide the avocado mixture between them, then sprinkle with the sesame seeds. Garnish with sprigs of mint. ·2·3·7·

Scottish Honey Posset

Metric/Imperial	American
3 tablespoons medium oatmeal	3 tablespoons medium oatmeal
6 tablespoons clear honey	6 tablespoons clear honey
grated rind and juice of 1 orange	grated rind and juice of 1 orange
2 tablespoons whisky	2 tablespoons whisky
300 ml/½ pint double or whipping cream	1¼ cups heavy or whipping cream
orange slices, to decorate	orange slices, to decorate

1. Spread the oatmeal evenly on a baking sheet and toast under a preheated medium hot grill (broiler) for 2 to 3 minutes until golden brown. Allow to cool before adding the liquid ingredients.
2. Place the honey, orange rind and juice, whisky and cream in a bowl. Lightly whip for about 3 to 5 minutes with an electric whisk.
3. Stir in the oatmeal and spoon into individual glasses. Decorate with orange slices and refrigerate until required. ·12·

Cook's Tip:
This Scottish Honey Posset is a less rich version of the Scottish Cranachan. Serve with a compote of fruit, such as raspberries, strawberries and redcurrants, if wished. If appetites are large a selection of shortbread biscuits can be offered with the posset.

Optional extra:
Instead of basil in the Cheesy Potatoes, use marjoram or oregano for a tasty difference. And try blue cheese instead of Cheddar. For the diet conscious, natural yogurt instead of double cream provides a healthy, less rich alternative for this supper dish.

C · O · U · N · T · D · O · W · N

To serve at 8 pm:
6.50: Preheat the oven.
7.00: Preheat the grill (broiler). Make up the Cheesy Potatoes and bake at the top of the oven.
7.10: Grill (broil) the oatmeal for the Scottish Honey Posset and cool. Prepare the Cidered Fish Bake and cook in the oven below the potatoes.
7.20: Combine all the ingredients for the Scottish Honey Posset, spoon into individual glasses, decorate and refrigerate.
7.30: Prepare the Avocado Sesame Salad. Cover and refrigerate.
7.40: Fry or toast the bread for the Chicken Liver Toasts and keep warm. Prepare and cook the chicken liver mixture.
7.50: Finish the Cidered Fish Bake.
8.00: Stir the lemon juice into the chicken liver mixture, spoon evenly over the croûtes, garnish and serve immediately.

F · R · E · E · Z · E · R · N · O · T · E · S

None of the dishes is suitable for freezing.

△ M·E·N·U △

· 10 ·

Saturday Supper for 4

Potted Cheese
·

Pork Chops with Juniper
Creamy Noodles with Fresh Herbs
Cabbage with Bacon
·

Rhubarb Fool with Shortbread Stars

Potted cheese is an economical starter: the addition of mustard, paprika and beer turns the full-fat cheese into something quite special. For more bite, use 1 tablespoon drained green peppercorns in place of the paprika. Finely grated Cheddar makes a tasty alternative to the full-fat cheese. (Potted cheese is also excellent picnic fare if served with crusty French bread.)

The juniper berries give flavour to the pork chops and the bacon adds a new dimension to cabbage. The cream added to the noodles is pure luxury but can be omitted if you are cooking on a budget. Drink a red or white wine of your choice with the pork.

Presenting the Food Well

Although a fairly informal meal, be imaginative with your presentation. This doesn't mean that you have to spend a fortune on tableware: it is the unexpected touch that makes a memorable impression on your guests, especially friends you entertain on a regular basis. Arrange the Potted Cheese and crackers, or toast on that large brass tray that usually stands on the hall table – protect it first by covering it with cling film (plastic wrap).

Potted Cheese

Metric/Imperial	American
150 g/5 oz unsalted butter	2/3 cup unsalted butter
250 g/8 oz full-fat soft cheese	1 cup full-fat curd cheese
1 teaspoon German mustard	1 teaspoon German mustard
4 teaspoons paprika	4 teaspoons paprika
2 tablespoons beer	2 tablespoons lager
1 teaspoon grated onion	1 teaspoon grated onion
1 teaspoon finely chopped chives	1 teaspoon finely chopped chives
salt	salt
freshly ground black pepper	freshly ground black pepper
sprigs of mint, to garnish	sprigs of mint, to garnish

1. Cream the butter in a bowl, or use a food processor, and then work in the remaining ingredients. Pack the mixture into individual pots and chill.
2. Garnish with sprigs of mint and serve with crackers or fingers of buttered toast. ·2·4·13·

Pork Chops with Juniper

Metric/Imperial	American
4 tablespoons olive oil	4 tablespoons olive oil
4 pork chops, about 250 g/8 oz each	4 pork chops, about 1/2 lb each
2 shallots, peeled and chopped	2 shallots, peeled and chopped
1 clove garlic, peeled and chopped	1 clove garlic, peeled and chopped
8 juniper berries, roughly crushed	8 juniper berries, roughly crushed
1 × 250 g/8 oz can tomatoes, chopped	1 × 8 oz can tomatoes, chopped
4 tablespoons gin or vodka	4 tablespoons gin or vodka
120 ml/4 fl oz chicken stock	1/2 cup chicken stock
	1/2 tablespoon chopped fresh

1/2 tablespoon chopped fresh thyme or 1/2 teaspoon dried	thyme or 1/2 teaspoon dried
salt	salt
freshly ground black pepper	freshly ground black pepper

1. Heat the oil in a deep frying pan (skillet) with a lid and fry the pork chops over a high heat for 3 to 4 minutes on each side to brown. Remove and keep warm.
2. Add the shallots to the pan and sauté over gentle heat for 2 minutes, then add the garlic and cook for 1 minute.
3. Stir in the juniper berries and tomatoes, and cook for 2 to 3 minutes, stirring. Add the gin and boil rapidly until reduced by half. Pour in the stock and stir in the thyme. Add salt and pepper to taste.
4. Return the pork chops to the pan, cover and simmer for 20 minutes, adding a little extra stock if necessary, until the chops are cooked through. ·2·4·

Creamy Noodles with Fresh Herbs

Metric/Imperial	American
450 g/1 lb tagliatelle	1 lb tagliatelle
2 cloves garlic, peeled and crushed	2 cloves garlic, peeled and crushed
50 g/2 oz butter	1/4 cup butter
120 ml/4 fl oz single cream	1/2 cup light cream
2 tablespoons chopped parsley	2 tablespoons chopped parsley
2 tablespoons snipped chives	2 tablespoons chopped chives
1 tablespoon chopped basil	1 tablespoon chopped basil
1 tablespoon chopped oregano or marjoram	1 tablespoon chopped oregano or marjoram
salt	salt
freshly ground black pepper	freshly ground black pepper

1. Cook the pasta in a saucepan of boiling salted

water for about 10 minutes until tender but still firm to the bite (*al dente*).

2. Drain thoroughly and toss with the crushed garlic and butter.

3. Heat the cream just to boiling point and add the chopped herbs, remove from heat. Add salt and pepper to taste.

4. Pour over the buttered pasta and toss gently but thoroughly until mixed. ·12·

Cabbage with Bacon

Metric/Imperial

4 streaky bacon rashers, diced
1 clove garlic, peeled and crushed

American

4 slices fatty bacon, diced
1 clove garlic, peeled and crushed
1 sprig of rosemary

1 sprig of rosemary
1 small Savoy cabbage, shredded
150 ml/1/4 pint chicken stock
salt
freshly ground black pepper

1 small Savoy cabbage, shredded
2/3 cup chicken stock
salt
freshly ground black pepper

1. Put the bacon, garlic and rosemary in a heavy-based frying pan (skillet) and sauté over moderate heat for 5 minutes until browned.

2. Lower the heat and add the shredded cabbage, stock and salt and pepper to taste. Cover and cook gently for 40 minutes, stirring frequently.

3. Transfer to a warm serving dish and serve. ·4·11·

Rhubarb fool

Rhubarb Fool

Metric/Imperial	American
500 g/1 lb rhubarb, coarsely chopped	1 lb rhubarb, coarsely chopped
50-75 g/2-3 oz demerara sugar	1/2 cup firmly packed brown sugar
grated rind of 1 small orange	grated rind of 1 small orange
150-250 ml/5-8 fl oz double cream, according to taste	1/2-1 cup heavy cream, according to taste
2 scant teaspoons Pernod	2 scant teaspoons Pernod
Shortbread Stars, to serve	Shortbread Stars, to serve

1. Gently simmer the rhubarb in a saucepan with a very little water, the sugar and orange rind until tender. (Do not overcook as it will lose its bright colour.)
2. Drain the rhubarb and cool completely.
3. Whip the cream until it just begins to hold its shape. Stir in the Pernod. Fold the flavoured cream into the rhubarb.
4. Serve in individual glasses with Shortbread Stars.
·9·12·

Shortbread Stars

Metric/Imperial	American
100 g/4 oz soft margarine	1/2 cup soft margarine
25 g/1 oz icing sugar, sieved	1/4 cup sifted confectioners' sugar
75 g/3 oz plain flour, sieved	3/4 cup sifted all-purpose flour
25 g/1 oz cornflour	1/4 cup cornstarch
few drops of vanilla essence	few drops of vanilla
glacé cherries to decorate	glacé cherries to decorate

1. Cream the margarine and icing (confectioners') sugar together until pale. Mix in the flour, cornflour (cornstarch) and vanilla.

2. Spoon the mixture into a piping (pastry) bag fitted with a 1 cm (1/2 inch) star nozzle. Pipe tiny stars on to a greased baking sheet and top each with a tiny piece of cherry.
3. Cook in a preheated oven (190°C/375°F), Gas Mark 5 for about 10 minutes until lightly golden. Transfer to a wire rack and leave until cold.

C · O · U · N · T · D · O · W · N
The day before:
Make the Shortbread Stars.
To serve at 8 pm:
6.00: Open the red wine, if using.
7.00: Chill the white wine, if using. Prepare the rhubarb for the fool. Cook and cool.
7.05: Prepare the Potted Cheese, spoon into individual dishes, garnish and refrigerate.
About 7.15: Prepare the Cabbage with Bacon and leave to cook.
7.25: Make up and cook the Pork Chops with Juniper. Complete the Rhubarb Fool, spoon into individual glasses and refrigerate.
7.50: Cook the noodles for the Creamy Noodles with Fresh Herbs. Prepare the remaining ingredients for the noodles and heat the cream.
7.55: If required, toast some bread to serve with the Potted Cheese. Transfer the cabbage to a serving dish.
8.00: Toss the noodles in the butter and garlic. Keep warm. Serve the Potted Cheese with crackers or toast fingers.

F · R · E · E · Z · E · R · N · O · T · E · S
Wrap and freeze the Potted Cheese at the end of stage 1. Thaw overnight in the refrigerator. Garnish as per recipe. Cool, pack and freeze the Pork Chops with Juniper at the end of stage 4. Thaw overnight in the refrigerator. Place in a casserole, cover and reheat at (190°C/350°F) Gas Mark 5 for 40 minutes. Add more stock if necessary. Pack and freeze the Rhubarb Fool at the end of stage 3. Thaw overnight.

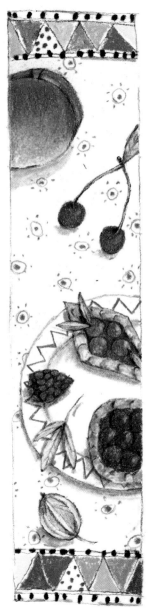

△ M · E · N · U △

· 11 ·

Low-cost Lunch for 4

Homestead Soup with Curried Croûtons

·

Parsleyed Calf's Liver
Green Beans with Cheese and Sage
Purée of Brussels Sprouts

·

Butterscotch Mousse

This economical warming lunch menu is perfect for family or friends. It is high in food value but low on cost.

Homemade Soups

These are superior to canned or packaged soups in both flavour and nutrients, and this recipe proves that they don't take hours to cook. The curried croûtons are effortless to make and give the soup additional flavour and texture. (The soup can be prepared well in advance if necessary and simply reheated when required.)

Healthy Eating

The combination of calf's (veal) liver and parsley makes the main course particularly healthy, rich in iron and vitamins. (Liver is not to everyone's taste so play safe and check with your guests in advance if necessary.) Calf's liver has an especially delicate flavour but lower priced lamb's liver can be used instead. The secret of delicious liver is not to overcook it: when served, it should still be slightly pink inside. A splash of dry white wine is used in the recipe to make it something special: chill the remainder and serve with the meal.

Homestead Soup with Curried Croûtons

Metric/Imperial	American
25 g/1 oz butter	2 tablespoons butter
2 large leeks, cleaned and chopped	2 large leeks, cleaned and chopped
4 medium carrots, diced	4 medium carrots, diced
4 celery sticks, diced	4 celery stalks, diced
1 × 396 g/14 oz can tomatoes	1 × 14 oz can tomatoes
750 ml/1¼ pints vegetable stock	3 cups vegetable stock
1 teaspoon Worcestershire sauce	1 teaspoon Worcestershire sauce
salt	salt
freshly ground black pepper	freshly ground black pepper
Croûtons:	Croûtons:
50 g/2 oz butter, softened	¼ cup softened butter
1 teaspoon curry powder	1 teaspoon curry powder
4 × 1 cm/½ inch thick slices white or brown bread	4 × ½ inch thick slices white or brown bread

1. Melt the butter in a large saucepan and sauté the leeks, carrots and celery for 5 minutes. Add the tomatoes and stock, bring to the boil.
2. Cover and simmer for 20 minutes or until the vegetables are soft. For a smoother texture, remove half the soup from the pan and purée in a blender or food processor. Return to the pan and reheat. Add the Worcestershire sauce and salt and pepper to taste.
3. For the croûtons, mix together the butter and curry powder. Toast the bread on one side. Spread the curried butter on the untoasted side and grill (broil) until crisp. Cut into 1 cm/½ inch cubes. Serve with the soup. ·10·12·14·

Variation:
Add 1 clove garlic, crushed to the softened butter to replace the curry powder.

Parsleyed Calf's Liver

Metric/Imperial	American
2 tablespoons plain flour	2 tablespoons all-purpose flour
salt	salt
freshly ground black pepper	freshly ground black pepper
4 large thin slices calf's liver, about 125 g/4 oz each	4 large thin slices veal liver, about ¼ lb each
25 g/1 oz butter	2 tablespoons butter
2 tablespoons olive oil	2 tablespoons olive oil
2 cloves garlic, peeled and finely chopped	2 cloves garlic, peeled and finely chopped
1-2 tablespoons white wine vinegar	1-2 tablespoons white wine vinegar
4 tablespoons dry white wine	4 tablespoons dry white wine
2 tablespoons chopped parsley	2 tablespoons chopped parsley

1. Spread the flour out on a large flat plate and add salt and pepper. Dip the liver slices in the seasoned flour to coat thoroughly.
2. Heat the butter and oil in a frying pan (skillet) and fry two liver slices over a moderate heat for about 2 minutes on each side or until the liver is still slightly pink in the centre.
3. Transfer the fried liver to a serving dish and keep warm. Fry the remaining liver in the same way and transfer to the serving dish.
4. Add the garlic to the pan and cook over a gentle heat, stirring often and adding a little more butter or oil if necessary, for about 1½ minutes. Add the vinegar and wine and swirl around the pan for 1 to 2 minutes. Stir in the parsley and pour the mixture over the liver. ·9·10·

Variation:
If serving this menu to children replace the dry white wine with 4 tablespoons of light stock. You may also want to omit the garlic. If so, try adding a tablespoon of grated orange rind.

Green Beans with Cheese and Sage

Metric/Imperial

500 g/1 lb French beans, trimmed
25 g/1 oz butter
1 tablespoon oil
2 tablespoons chopped sage
1 clove garlic, crushed
good pinch of grated nutmeg
salt
freshly ground black pepper
2 tablespoons freshly grated Parmesan cheese

American

1 lb green beans, trimmed
2 tablespoons butter
1 tablespoon oil
2 tablespoons chopped sage
1 clove garlic, crushed
good pinch of grated nutmeg
salt
freshly ground black pepper
2 tablespoons freshly grated Parmesan cheese

1. Cook the beans in a saucepan of boiling salted water until just tender, then drain.
2. Heat the butter and oil in a saucepan, stir in 1 tablespoon of the chopped sage and the garlic. Cook for 1 minute, stirring, then add the beans, nutmeg, and salt and pepper to taste.
3. Stir for another 1 to 2 minutes over a gentle heat, then add the grated cheese and lightly stir through. Turn into a warm serving dish and sprinkle with the remaining parsley. ·4·14·

Variation:

Try using fresh basil in place of the 2 tablespoons of chopped sage. A scattering of sesame seeds may also add an interesting texture to this vegetable dish.

Homestead soup with curried croûtons

Purée of Brussels Sprouts

Metric/Imperial	American
salt	salt
750 g/1½ lb Brussels sprouts, trimmed	1½ lb Brussels sprouts, trimmed
50 g/2 oz butter	¼ cup butter
1 clove garlic, peeled and crushed	1 clove garlic, peeled and crushed
¼ teaspoon grated nutmeg	¼ teaspoon grated nutmeg
freshly ground black pepper	freshly ground black pepper
3 tablespoons double cream	3 tablespoons heavy cream

1. Bring 2.5 cm/1 inch salted water to the boil in a large saucepan. Add the sprouts and cook, uncovered, for 6 to 8 minutes or until the sprouts are very tender. Drain.

2. Purée the sprouts in a blender or food processor for about 30 seconds, depending on whether a coarse or fine purée is wanted.

3. Melt the butter in the rinsed out pan and sauté the garlic for 1 minute. Return the puréed sprouts, and stir well to coat in butter. Add the nutmeg and salt and pepper to taste. Heat through over a low heat for 2 minutes, shaking the pan once or twice.

4. Stir in 2 tablespoons of the cream and transfer to a warm serving dish. Garnish with the remaining cream. ·4·10·

Variation:

For a hot vegetable bake, beat 2 egg yolks into the sprout purée. Fold in 2 whisked egg whites and bake in a preheated oven (200°C/400°F), Gas Mark 6 for 25 minutes.

Butterscotch Mousse

Metric/Imperial	American
600 ml/1 pint milk	2½ cups milk
40 g/1½ oz cornflour	generous ¼ cup cornstarch
175 g/6 oz demerara sugar	1 cup firmly packed brown sugar
2 eggs, separated	2 eggs, separated
1 teaspoon vanilla essence	1 teaspoon vanilla
instant coffee granules, to decorate	instant coffee granules, to decorate

1. Blend a little of the milk with the cornflour (cornstarch) in a saucepan to give a smooth paste. Add the remaining milk and cook, stirring, over a gentle heat until the mixture has thickened. Simmer, stirring, for 1 minute.

2. Dissolve the sugar in a pan over medium heat until liquid. Do not stir. Remove from the heat, cool slightly, then carefully stir into the milk sauce with the egg yolks. Beat until smooth. Cool slightly, then add the vanilla.

3. Whisk the egg whites until stiff and fold into the sauce. Pour into a serving dish and chill. Sprinkle with coffee granules just before serving. ·7·10·

C·O·U·N·T·D·O·W·N

To serve at 1 pm:

12.00: Chill the white wine. Prepare the soup.

12.10: Prepare and cook the Brussels sprouts.

12.15: Make the Butterscotch Mousse.

12.25: Purée the sprouts until smooth.

12.30: Purée half the soup until smooth. Keep warm.

12.35: Prepare the French (green) beans and new potatoes. Make the curried croûtons and set aside.

12.40: Cook the green beans and the potatoes. Finish the puréed sprouts.

12.45: Trim, slice and fry the liver.

12.50: Drain the green beans, toss in the cheese mixture and keep warm.

12.55: Complete the Parsleyed Calf's Liver.

1.00: Serve the soup.

F·R·E·E·Z·E·R·N·O·T·E·S

Cool, pack and freeze the soup at the end of stage 2. Thaw overnight in the refrigerator. Bring to the boil and simmer gently for 5 to 10 minutes to reheat.

△ M·E·N·U △

· 12 ·

Spring Dinner for 4

Beetroot Soup with Cumin

·

Veal with Mushroom Sauce
Green Noodles with Tarragon Butter
Spring Vegetable Casserole

·

Poached Liqueur Pears

This is another relatively inexpensive dinner party menu with an air of spring about it.

Colourful Food

The colourful beetroot soup is unusual and far quicker to prepare than the more traditional Bortsch. Although you can serve the soup with rolls, try accompanying it with warmed pitta bread. The pears in white wine and blackcurrants turn a beautiful rich crimson colour; if time allows, make in advance and serve them chilled.

For Economy

The veal main course can be made equally well with veal or pork chops but these will require a little longer to cook. If you have difficulty obtaining tarragon, flavour the butter with 1 tablespoon capers instead. Finally, if you don't have time to prepare the Spring Vegetable Casserole, simply serve a green vegetable like steamed courgettes (zucchini), broccoli or green beans.

Veal is complemented by red or white wine, so choose from a Bordeaux or a German white Piesporter or Bernkasteler.

Beetroot Soup with Cumin

Metric/Imperial	American
4 medium-sized raw beetroots, peeled and cubed	4 medium-sized raw beets, peeled and cubed
450 ml/3/4 pint water	2 cups water
1 teaspoon cumin seeds	1 teaspoon cumin seeds
10 black peppercorns	10 black peppercorns
4 cloves	4 cloves
2.5 cm/1 inch piece of cinnamon stick	1 inch piece of cinnamon stick
7 g/1/4 oz butter	1/2 tablespoon butter
1/2 tablespoon vegetable oil	1/2 tablespoon vegetable oil
1 × 250 g/8 oz can tomatoes	1 × 8 oz can tomatoes
1 teaspoon salt	1 teaspoon salt
4 tablespoons single or soured cream	4 tablespoons light or sour cream
4 sprigs of sage, to garnish	4 sprigs of sage, to garnish
hot pitta bread, to serve	hot pitta bread, to serve

1. Put the beetroot with the water in a blender or food processor and work for 1 minute. Turn into a fine sieve set over a bowl and extract as much of the juice as possible, pressing with the back of a wooden spoon.
2. Tie the spices together in a piece of muslin (cheesecloth) and crush lightly. Heat the butter and oil in a saucepan over a moderate heat and add the spice bag, tomatoes with their juice and beetroot. Bring to the boil, cover and simmer for 25 minutes. Remove and discard the spice bag.
3. Blend the soup in a blender or food processor, if liked.
4. Just before serving, add the salt, then the cream. Stir well to mix, then reheat. Do this very gently to avoid curdling the mixture.
5. Ladle the soup into warm soup bowls or cups, garnish with sage and serve with hot pitta bread. ·4·14·

Veal with Mushroom Sauce

Metric/Imperial	American
4 veal escalopes, about 125 g/4 oz each	4 veal scaloppine, about 1/4 lb each
1/4 teaspoon ground turmeric	1/4 teaspoon ground turmeric
salt	salt
freshly ground black pepper	freshly ground black pepper
150 ml/1/4 pint dry white vermouth, sherry or white wine	2/3 cup dry white vermouth, sherry or white wine
300 ml/1/2 pint double cream	2-3 tablespoons butter
about 25 g/1 oz butter	1 1/4 cups heavy cream
50 g/2 oz button mushrooms, finely sliced	1/2 cup finely sliced button mushrooms
1 tablespoon French mustard	1 tablespoon Dijon mustard

1. If time allows, place the escalopes in a single layer in a shallow dish. Sprinkle with the turmeric and salt and pepper, then pour over the vermouth, sherry or wine. Cover and chill.
2. Put the cream in a heavy-based saucepan with a pinch of salt and bring slowly to the boil. As soon as it reaches boiling point, lower the heat and simmer gently, stirring frequently for 10 to 15 minutes until the cream becomes thick and golden.
3. Drain the escalopes. Gradually whisk the marinade into the cream, over a very low heat, until the sauce thickens slightly.
4. Meanwhile, melt the butter in a frying pan (skillet) and fry the escalopes briskly for about 3 minutes on each side until browned.
5. Add the mushrooms to the pan and sauté for 1 to 2 minutes over high heat. Remove from the pan with a slotted spoon and scatter over the escalopes.
6. Whisk the mustard into the cream sauce. Pour over the veal and mushrooms. ·4·10·

Green Noodles with Tarragon Butter

Metric/Imperial	American
2 cloves garlic, peeled and crushed	2 cloves garlic, peeled and crushed
125 g/4 oz butter, softened	½ cup softened butter
1 teaspoon lemon juice	1 teaspoon lemon juice
½ teaspoon grated lemon rind	½ teaspoon grated lemon rind
1 tablespoon chopped tarragon	1 tablespoon chopped tarragon
salt	salt
freshly ground black pepper	freshly ground black pepper
1 tablespoon vegetable oil	1 tablespoon vegetable oil
350 g/12 oz tagliatelle	¾ lb tagliatelle

1. To make the tarragon butter, beat the garlic into the butter. Gradually add the lemon juice, then beat in the lemon rind and tarragon.
2. Bring a large saucepan of water to the boil, add the salt and oil, lower in the noodles. Stir to separate them. Cover the pan and simmer for 10 minutes or until the noodles are 'al dente' – tender but still firm to the bite. Drain in a colander and pour hot water through them. Drain thoroughly.
3. Turn the noodles into a warm serving dish. Add the tarragon butter and toss to coat the noodles evenly. ·9·

Variation:
For a more colourful dish, use a combination of egg and spinach noodles.

Veal with mushroom sauce

Q·U·I·C·K · & · E·A·S·Y

Poached Liqueur Pears

Metric/Imperial	American
300 ml/½ pint medium or sweet white wine	*1¼ cups medium or sweet white wine*
125 g/4 oz blackcurrants, stalks removed	*1 cup black currants, stalks removed*
4 tablespoons honey	*¼ cup honey*
1 cinnamon stick	*1 cinnamon stick*
2 strips of lemon rind	*2 strips of lemon rind*
4-6 pears	*4-6 pears*
1 teaspoon arrowroot	*1 teaspoon arrowroot*
1 tablespoon crème de cassis	*1 tablespoon crème de cassis*

1. Pour the wine into a saucepan, then add the blackcurrants, honey, cinnamon and lemon rind. Heat gently until the honey has dissolved, then bring to the boil. Boil for 1 minute.

2. Peel the pears, leaving the stalks attached. Put the pears in the pan, submerging them as much as possible in the wine mixture. Cover and cook gently for about 20 minutes until the pears are tender, turning occasionally.

3. Lift the pears carefully out of the pan and transfer to a serving bowl. Discard the cinnamon stick and lemon rind.

4. Blend the arrowroot with a little cold water, then pour into the wine mixture. Bring to the boil, then lower the heat and simmer for 1 minute or until the sauce thickens, stirring constantly. Add the crème de cassis. Pour the sauce over the pears. Serve hot or chilled. ·1·4·10·

Variation:

Raspberries and Kirsch, or strawberries and Cointreau, would be delicious alternatives to use in this recipe.

Try serving Poached Liqueur Pears with a cinnamon cream. Lightly whip 150 ml/¼ pint double (heavy) cream with a pinch of ground cinnamon and 2 teaspoons soft light brown sugar. Chill for 20 to 30 minutes before serving.

C·O·U·N·T·D·O·W·N

On the day:

Make the dessert, if serving, and chill.

To serve at 8 pm:

6.00: Open the red wine, if using.

7.00: Chill the white wine, if using. Marinate the veal escalopes. Cover and chill.

7.05: Prepare and cook the soup.

7.15: Prepare the pears and poach for 20 minutes.

7.25: Sauté the onion and spring onion for the Spring Vegetable Casserole for 5 minutes. Meanwhile prepare the remaining vegetables. Complete the casserole, cover and simmer.

7.35: Purée the beetroot soup and reheat gently, without boiling. Bring the cream for the veal sauce to simmering point.

7.40: Thicken and finish the vegetable casserole. Preheat the grill (broiler) to moderate.

7.45: Fry the veal escalopes. Transfer to a serving dish and complete the dish; keep warm.

7.50: Cook the noodles and prepare the tarragon butter. Complete the dessert.

8.00: Drain the noodles, toss in the tarragon butter. Garnish the soup and serve.

F·R·E·E·Z·E·R · N·O·T·E·S

Cool, pack and freeze the beetroot soup at the end of stage 2. Finish as per recipe. The tarragon butter served with the noodles is a standard herb butter recipe. It is worth making in large quantities for future use. Once you have combined all the ingredients, position the mixture between two sheets of greaseproof (waxed) paper and roll into a sausage shape. Refrigerate until solid. Slice into 5 mm/¼ inch slices, pack into an airtight container and freeze. Remove pats of the herb butter when you need them, to serve on vegetables, steaks, baked potatoes or fish. Any fresh herbs can be used in place of the tarragon. Cool, pack and freeze the Poached Liqueur Pears at the end of stage 4. Thaw overnight in the refrigerator. Reheat gently if wished.

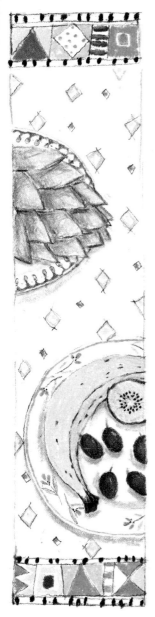

△ M·E·N·U ▲

· 13 ·

Casual Lunch for 6

Lemon Butter Mushrooms
Herb Soda Bread

·

Lamb Chops with Rosemary
or Mediterranean Fennel Casserole
Courgette and Cheese Bake

·

Chocolate Layered Crunch

This homely menu is perfect for those days when good friends come round and you don't want to spend your time in the kitchen.

For Speed

If time is short opt for the lamb chops rather than the fennel casserole with fish. For a two-course meal simply serve the Lemon Butter Mushrooms as a vegetable in place of the more elaborate Courgette Cheese Bake. The quick-to-make Herb Soda Bread requires no yeast and no kneading so it is ideal for those occasions when you are caught with no bread in the house. For a different flavour, omit the herbs and use beer (lager) in place of the milk. Only make a small quantity of soda bread, as it does not keep well and is best eaten on the day it is made, served warm with lots of butter.

Choice of Wine

When you have decided on your main course, choosing an appropriate wine becomes easy. Drink a good red Bordeaux with the lamb or a white wine, Graves, with the casserole.

Lemon Butter Mushrooms

Metric/Imperial	American
500 g/1 lb button mushrooms	1 lb button mushrooms
50 g/2 oz butter	1/4 cup butter
4 tablespoons lemon juice	4 tablespoons lemon juice
1 teaspoon grated lemon rind	1 teaspoon grated lemon rind
freshly ground black pepper	freshly ground black pepper
1 tablespoon chopped parsley	1 tablespoon chopped parsley

1. Wipe the mushrooms with damp absorbent kitchen paper and place in a saucepan with the butter, lemon juice, rind and plenty of pepper.
2. Cover the pan, bring to the boil and simmer for 5 minutes. Serve sprinkled with parsley either as a starter with piping hot Herb Soda Bread or as a vegetable accompaniment the main dish. ·3·4·12·

Lemon butter mushrooms

Herb Soda Bread

Metric/Imperial	American
25 g/1 oz fresh mixed herbs, leaves only (marjoram, parsley, chives, basil and rosemary) or 1 teaspoon dried mixed herbs	1 oz fresh mixed herbs, leaves only (marjoram, parsley, chives, basil and rosemary) or 1 teaspoon dried mixed herbs
125 g/4 oz wholemeal flour	1 cup wholewheat flour
125 g/4 oz plain flour, sifted	1 cup all-purpose flour, sifted
1/2 teaspoon bicarbonate of soda	1/2 teaspoon baking soda
1/2 teaspoon salt	1/2 teaspoon salt
50 g/2 oz butter, cut into pieces	1/4 cup butter, cut into pieces
1 teaspoon cream of tartar	1 teaspoon cream of tartar
150 ml/1/4 pint milk	2/3 cup milk
1 egg, beaten	1 egg, beaten
1 teaspoon caraway seeds	1 teaspoon caraway seeds

1. Chop the herbs and place in a bowl with the flours, soda and salt. Mix well. Rub (cut) in the butter and mix thoroughly.
2. Stir the cream of tartar into the milk. Add to the bowl and blend until the mixture just forms a ball.
3. Knead lightly on a floured surface into a round shape. Brush the top with the egg, then sprinkle over the caraway seeds. Cut into four pieces.
4. Place on a floured baking sheet. Bake in a preheated oven (200°C/400°F), Gas Mark 6 for about 25 minutes. Tap the bottom – if it sounds hollow it is cooked. Cool on a wire rack.

Lamb Chops with Rosemary

Metric/Imperial	American
50 g/2 oz butter, softened	1/4 cup softened butter
6 lamb loin chops	6 lamb rib chops
chopped rosemary	chopped rosemary
freshly ground black pepper	freshly ground black pepper

1. Spread a little of the butter on each lamb chop. Sprinkle with rosemary and pepper.
2. Place the chops under a preheated hot grill (broiler) and grill (broil) for 7 minutes on each side.
3. Transfer the lamb chops to a warm serving plate and serve.

Mediterranean Fennel Casserole

Metric/Imperial	American
3 heads of fennel	3 heads fennel
40 g/1 1/2 oz butter	3 tablespoons butter
3 cloves garlic, peeled and halved	3 cloves garlic, peeled and halved
275 g/10 oz mushrooms	2 1/2 cups mushrooms
350 g/12 oz tomatoes,	3/4 lb tomatoes, peeled and
skinned and quartered	quartered
450 ml/3/4 pint meat stock	2 cups meat stock
350 g/12 oz white fish fillets, e.g. cod, haddock	3/4 lb white fish fillets, e.g. cod, haddock
salt	salt
freshly ground black pepper	freshly ground black pepper
2 tablespoons tomato purée	2 tablespoons tomato paste
2 teaspoons made mustard	2 teaspoons made mustard
2 tablespoons double cream	2 tablespoons heavy cream
2 tablespoons chopped mixed herbs	2 tablespoons chopped mixed herbs

1. Remove the stalks and leaves from the fennel and cut the heads into quarters or large pieces. Melt the butter in a saucepan and sauté the garlic until brown.
2. Add the mushrooms, tomatoes and fennel to the garlic butter and cook, over a low heat, for 4 to 5 minutes. Add the stock, stirring well.
3. Cut the fish into 2.5 cm/1 inch cubes or strips and add to the pan. Add salt and pepper to taste and simmer gently for about 15 minutes.
4. Add the tomato purée, mustard and cream, if using, blending well. Transfer to a warm serving dish and sprinkle with chopped herbs before serving.

Courgette and Cheese Bake

Metric/Imperial	American
500 g/1 lb tomatoes, skinned and chopped or 1 × 400 g/14 oz can chopped tomatoes	2 cups peeled, chopped tomatoes or 1 × 1 lb can chopped tomatoes
1 small onion, chopped	1 small onion, chopped
salt	salt
freshly ground black pepper	freshly ground black pepper
750 g/1 1/2 lb courgettes, coarsely chopped	1 1/2 lb zucchini, coarsely chopped
2 tablespoons plain flour	2 tablespoons all-purpose flour
25 g/1 oz butter	2 tablespoons butter
250 g/8 oz Edam cheese, thinly sliced	1/2 lb Edam cheese, thinly sliced

1. Put the tomatoes and onion in a saucepan, add salt and pepper to taste and cook for 10 minutes, stirring, until thick.
2. Coat the courgettes (zucchini) in the flour, shaking off any excess. Sauté the courgettes until brown in the butter.
3. Make layers of courgette, tomato mixture and cheese in a shallow casserole, finishing with a layer of cheese.
4. Bake in a preheated oven (200°C/400°F), Gas Mark 6 for 25 minutes.

Chocolate Layered Crunch

Metric/Imperial	American
125 g/4 oz wholemeal breadcrumbs	2 cups wholewheat bread crumbs
125 g/4 oz demerara sugar	2/3 cup firmly packed brown sugar
6 tablespoons drinking chocolate powder	6 tablespoons drinking chocolate powder
2 teaspoons instant coffee powder	2 teaspoons instant coffee powder
250 ml/8 fl oz whipping cream	1 cup whipping cream
6 tablespoons black cherry or strawberry jam	6 tablespoons black cherry or strawberry jam

1. Combine the breadcrumbs, sugar, chocolate and coffee powder in a bowl. Mix well to ensure the breadcrumbs are thoroughly coated in the sugar, chocolate and coffee.
2. Lightly whip the cream.
3. Spoon 1 tablespoon jam into each of six individual dishes, then arrange layers of cream and breadcrumb mixture, finishing with a layer of breadcrumb mixture and a spoonful of cream. Chill well before serving.

Variation:
For a delicious iced dessert, layer the breadcrumbs and cream mixture in six individual or 1 large freezer-proof container. Place in the freezer for 30 minutes.

C · O · U · N · T · D · O · W · N

On the day:
Make up the dessert, chill.
To serve at 1 pm:
11.00: Open the red wine, if using.
11.45: Preheat the oven to (200°C/400°F), Gas Mark 6. Chill the white wine, if using.
12.00: Scrub 6 medium-sized potatoes, prick them and rub with oil. Bake in the oven.
12.05: Prepare the Herb Soda Bread and bake in the oven above the potatoes.
12.15: Prepare and cook the tomatoes and onion for the Courgette and Cheese Bake. Prepare the courgettes (zucchini) and slice the cheese.
12.25: Fry the courgettes. Finish the dish and bake in the oven alongside the potatoes.
12.35: If serving the Mediterranean Fennel Casserole, prepare and cook the vegetables, add the fish and simmer for 15 minutes.
12.40: Preheat the grill (broiler) for the lamb chops.
About 12.45: If serving the lamb, spread the butter over the chops and place under the hot grill, turning them after about 7 minutes. Prepare the Lemon Butter Mushrooms.
12.55: Finish the fennel casserole, garnish and keep warm.
1.00: Transfer the chops to a serving dish and keep warm. Serve the Lemon Butter Mushrooms with the Herb Soda Bread.

F · R · E · E · Z · E · R · N · O · T · E · S

Cool, pack and freeze the Lemon Butter Mushrooms at the end of stage 2. Thaw overnight in the refrigerator. Simmer for 2 to 3 minutes before serving.
Cool, pack and freeze the Herb Soda Bread at the end of stage 4. Thaw overnight at cool room temperature. Wrap in foil and reheat in a preheated oven (200°C/400°F) Gas Mark 6 for 10 minutes.
Freeze the Chocolate Layered Crunch at the end of stage 3. Thaw overnight in the refrigerator.

⟁ M · E · N · U ⟁

· 14 ·

Celebration Dinner for 6

Mushroom and Sherry Soup

·

Chicken and Banana Supremes
French Beans in Tomato Sauce

·

Chocolate Cherry Pots

What better way is there to celebrate any occasion than with a beautifully prepared and presented meal? This celebration menu takes a little longer to prepare than other menus in this book, but it is worth every minute spent. Preparing ahead and freezing the soup will free you to spend more time getting the detail of your presentation right. Plan to do as much as possible beforehand.

Food Presentation

The presentation of food is all-important and the simpler the better. Plates should never be overfilled: nowadays the trend is towards small quantities of elegantly prepared food that shows itself off without the help of radish roses or tomato waterlilies. Usually just a herb sprig or sprinkling of fresh herbs, finely sliced orange, lemon or lime slices, fresh watercress or celery greens are all that is required to bring out the best in a dish.

Wine note

Serve a well-chilled fino sherry with the soup, rather than wine. A light, fruity French white such as Muscadet would be suitable to follow with the chicken.

Mushroom and Sherry Soup

Metric/Imperial
25 g/1 oz butter
1 onion, chopped
250 g/8 oz button
  mushrooms, thinly sliced
900 ml/1½ pints chicken
  or vegetable stock
1 teaspoon lemon juice
1 teaspoon fresh thyme or
  ½ teaspoon dried
salt
freshly ground black pepper
2 tablespoons dry or
  medium sherry
2 tablespoons chopped
  parsley, to garnish

American
2 tablespoons butter
1 onion, chopped
2 cups thinly sliced button
  mushrooms
4 cups chicken or vegetable
  stock
1 teaspoon lemon juice
1 teaspoon fresh thyme or
  ½ teaspoon dried
salt
freshly ground black pepper
2 tablespoons dry or cream
  sherry
2 tablespoons chopped
  parsley, to garnish

1. Melt the butter in a saucepan and sauté the onion for 5 minutes until lightly browned. Add the mushrooms and sauté for 2 minutes.
2. Pour in the stock and add the lemon juice, thyme and salt and pepper to taste. Bring to the boil and simmer for 5 minutes.
3. Stir in the sherry and garnish with parsley. Serve hot with warm bread rolls. ·4·12·13·

Chicken and Banana Supremes

Metric/Imperial
6 boned and skinned
  chicken breasts
2 tablespoons seasoned flour
25 g/1 oz butter
3 bananas, mashed
grated rind of ½ lemon

American
6 boned and skinned
  chicken breasts
2 tablespoons seasoned flour
2 tablespoons butter
3 bananas, mashed
grated rind of ½ lemon

squeeze of lemon juice
3 tablespoons ground
  hazelnuts
salt
freshly ground black pepper
6 slices of Parma ham
Sauce:
6 tablespoons natural
  yogurt
2 tablespoons dry white
  wine
1 tablespoon chopped basil
To Garnish:
2 bananas, sliced
clear honey
flaked hazelnuts
sprigs of basil

squeeze of lemon juice
3 tablespoons ground
  hazelnuts
salt
freshly ground black pepper
6 slices of Parma ham
Sauce:
6 tablespoons unflavored
  yogurt
2 tablespoons dry white
  wine
1 tablespoon chopped basil
To Garnish:
2 bananas, sliced
runny honey
flaked hazelnuts
sprigs of basil

1. Dust the chicken breasts in seasoned flour. Melt the butter in a large shallow pan and fry the chicken breasts until evenly coloured on both sides and almost tender. Drain the chicken breasts on absorbent kitchen paper; reserve the cooking juices.
2. Mix the mashed banana with the lemon rind and juice, ground hazelnuts and salt and pepper to taste.
3. Spoon some of the banana mixture onto one side of each chicken breast, then wrap in a slice of ham.
4. Place the wrapped chicken breasts in a lightly greased ovenproof dish. Spoon over the reserved cooking juices and cover with foil. Cook in a preheated oven (190°C/375°F), Gas Mark 5 for 12 minutes.
5. To make the sauce, mix all the ingredients together in a saucepan and heat gently.
6. To make the garnish, spread the banana slices lightly with the honey, then dip into the nuts.
7. Spoon the basic sauce over the chicken breasts. Garnish the dish with sprigs of fresh basil before serving. ·1·4·10·

Chicken and banana supremes

French Beans in Tomato Sauce

Metric/Imperial	American
500 g/1 lb French beans	1 lb green beans
salt	salt
2 tablespoons olive oil	2 tablespoons olive oil
1 onion, roughly chopped	1 onion, roughly chopped
2 cloves garlic, peeled and crushed	2 cloves garlic, peeled and crushed
1 tablespoon chopped parsley	1 tablespoon chopped parsley
1 × 400 g/14 oz can tomatoes, chopped	1 × 14 oz can tomatoes, chopped
1 teaspoon ground cumin	1 teaspoon ground cumin
1 tablespoon wine vinegar	1 tablespoon wine vinegar
freshly ground black pepper	freshly ground black pepper
celery leaves, to garnish	celery leaves, to garnish

1. Cook the beans in a saucepan of boiling salted water for about 10 minutes until tender. Drain.

2. Heat the oil in a large saucepan and gently sauté the onion, garlic and parsley for about 5 minutes.

3. Stir in the tomatoes with their juice, the cumin and wine vinegar. Cook for about 30 minutes, then sieve. Season.

4. Transfer the beans to a serving dish and pour over the sauce. Garnish with celery leaves. ·4·11·

Variation:

Any seasonal green vegetables can be treated in this way. Try courgettes, marrow, broad beans or runner beans. A mixture of fresh herbs could be used if available. A combination of parsley and chives, or rosemary and thyme would be equally successful. Canned tomatoes have been used for convenience and speed but 225 g/8 oz of fresh tomatoes can be substituted.

Chocolate Cherry Pots

Metric/Imperial

1 × 425 g/15 oz can
  stoned black cherries,
  drained
125 g/4 oz plain chocolate
4 eggs, separated
25 g/1 oz butter
3 tablespoons Kirsch or
  brandy
To Decorate:
150 ml/5 fl oz double or
  whipping cream,
  whipped
chocolate curls
sponge fingers, to serve

American

1 × 15 oz can pitted bing
  cherries, drained
4 squares semi-sweet
  chocolate
4 eggs, separated
2 tablespoons butter
3 tablespoons Kirsch or
  brandy
To Decorate:
2/3 cup heavy or whipping
  cream, whipped
chocolate curls
lady fingers, to serve

1. Divide the cherries between six small individual
deep dishes.
2. Break the chocolate into pieces and place in a
bowl. Stand the bowl over a saucepan of hot water
until the chocolate has melted.
3. Remove the chocolate from the heat and beat in
the egg yolks, butter and Kirsch or brandy.
4. Whisk the egg whites stiffly and fold lightly but
thoroughly into the chocolate mixture. Spoon into
the dishes and chill.
5. Just before serving, decorate the pots with
whipped cream and chocolate curls. Serve with
sponge (lady) fingers. ·1·9·

Chocolate Curls

The Easy Way Take small pieces of chocolate and
scrape curls off with a potato peeler.

The Professional Way Spread melted chocolate on a
cool dry surface; marble is the best, but a Formica
chopping board will do. Keep the surface of the
chocolate as smooth as possible. Leave the chocolate
to set. Using a large sharp kitchen knife held at a 45°
angle, push the knife away from you along the
chocolate. The chocolate will roll and form curls.

C·O·U·N·T·D·O·W·N

To serve at 8 pm:

6.40: Make up the Chocolate Cherry Pots and
refrigerate. Whip the cream, spoon into a piping bag
and refrigerate. Prepare the chocolate curls, cover
and set aside either in the refrigerator or freezer
compartment. Keep cool until just before serving.

6.55: Chill the sherry and white wine. Prepare the
tomato sauce to serve with the green beans. Trim the
beans.

7.05: Prepare and fry the chicken breasts until
almost tender. Meanwhile, prepare the banana
filling.

7.20: Spoon the banana filling into the chicken
breasts. Wrap in Parma ham. Place on a baking sheet
and set aside.

7.30: Preheat the oven.

About 7.35: Prepare and sauté the onion and
mushrooms for the soup. Add the stock and
seasoning and simmer. Cook the green beans until
just tender.

7.45: Place the chicken supremes in the oven.
Prepare the sauce and garnish for the chicken. Drain
the beans, adjust the flavour of the tomato sauce and
mix into the beans. Cover the French Beans in
Tomato Sauce and keep warm.

7.55: Complete the Chicken and Banana Supremes.
Keep warm.

8.00: Stir the sherry into the soup, garnish with
chopped parsley.

Between courses: Remove the dessert from the refrigerator and decorate the Chocolate Cherry Pots with the
cream and chocolate curls.

F·R·E·E·Z·E·R · N·O·T·E·S

Cool, pack and freeze the Mushroom and Sherry Soup
at the end of stage 2. Thaw overnight in the
refrigerator. Bring to the boil, simmer for 5 minutes
and garnish as per recipe. Open freeze the chocolate
curls for the Chocolate Cherry Pots. Use from frozen
when required.

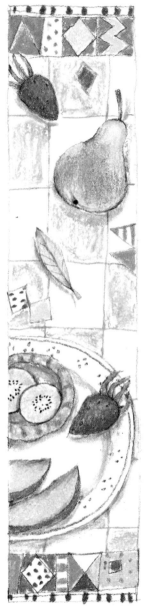

⊿ M · E · N · U ⊿

· 15 ·

Sunday Lunch for 4

Asparagus Parmesan

·

Country Lamb

·

Ginger Orange Trifle

This quick and easy Sunday lunch menu highlights the usefulness of a well-stocked store cupboard, particularly for the starter and dessert. When there are large appetites to cater for, this meal can be put together and served in just 45 minutes.

For Ease

Canned asparagus can be the basis of many attractive and appetizing starters. Serve it hot with eggs as in this menu, or topped with a sauce made from sautéed onion and canned tomatoes – sprinkle over some crushed crisps (chips) to give the dish crunch; or simply top it with a rich cheese sauce and brown under a grill (broiler). For a summer lunch, serve asparagus cold topped with a hollandaise sauce.

To Glaze Carrots

Simply peel and slice about 500 g/1 lb carrots. Place in a heavy-based saucepan with about 50 g/2 oz (¼ cup) butter and 1 tablespoon brown sugar. Cover tightly and cook very slowly without removing the lid for 20 minutes. Check to see if they are tender, then cook uncovered for a little longer until any liquid has evaporated.

Red wine is the best partner for lamb dishes: choose a Saint-Emilion or Pomerol.

Asparagus Parmesan

Metric/Imperial	American
2 × 275 g/10 oz cans asparagus	2 × 10 oz cans asparagus
50 g/2 oz butter	4 tablespoons butter
4 eggs	4 eggs
salt	salt
freshly ground black pepper	freshly ground black pepper
50 g/2 oz grated Parmesan cheese, to garnish	1/2 cup grated Parmesan cheese, to garnish

1. Heat the asparagus in its juice, drain and transfer the spears to four serving dishes.
2. Melt 25 g/1 oz (2 tablespoons) of the butter in a large frying pan (skillet) and cook until it turns golden brown. (This will only take a minute. Be careful not to burn the butter.)
3. Break the eggs into the pan and sprinkle with salt and pepper. Cook until the egg whites have set. Place one egg on each dish of asparagus.
4. Melt the remaining butter and pour over the asparagus. Sprinkle with Parmesan and serve immediately with wholemeal (wholewheat) rolls. ·9·10·11·

Country Lamb

Metric/Imperial	American
750 g/1 1/2 lb boned shoulder of lamb	1 1/2 lb boned square-cut shoulder lamb
2 teaspoons seasoned flour	2 teaspoons seasoned flour
50 g/2 oz butter	1/4 cup butter
1 × 396 g/14 oz can tomatoes, drained, juice reserved	1 × 14 oz can tomatoes, drained, juice reserved
350 g/12 oz courgettes, sliced	2 cups sliced zucchini
3 tablespoons chopped mint	3 tablespoons chopped mint
salt	salt
freshly ground black pepper	freshly ground black pepper

1. Trim any excess fat off the lamb. Cut the lamb into 2.5 cm/1 inch cubes and toss in the seasoned flour.
2. Melt the butter in a large saucepan and sauté the lamb until lightly browned.
3. Chop the tomatoes and add to the lamb with 4 tablespoons of the reserved tomato juice and the courgettes (zucchini). Cover the pan, reduce the heat and simmer for about 30 to 40 minutes or until the lamb is tender.
4. Stir in the mint and add salt and pepper to taste. Cook for a few more minutes. Serve with potatoes and carrots. ·2·9·

Variation:

For convenience, 8 lamb loin chops (rib chops) can be used in this recipe. Brown and cook as above.

Ginger Orange Trifle

Metric/Imperial	American
6 oranges	6 oranges
1 × 500 g/1 lb ginger cake	1 × 1 lb ginger cake
600 ml/1 pint packaged or canned custard	2 1/2 cups packaged or canned English dessert sauce
whipped cream, to decorate	whipped cream, to decorate

1. Peel 3 of the oranges of all skin and pith and slice the flesh very thinly. Remove any pips. Line the sides of a glass bowl or dish with the orange slices.
2. Slice the ginger cake. Squeeze the juice from 2 of the remaining oranges and sprinkle over the cake. Arrange the cake on top of the orange slices.
3. Pour the prepared custard into the bowl and smooth the top.
4. Peel and cut the remaining orange of all skin and pith. With a serrated knife cut into segments and use to decorate the top of the trifle, together with a little whipped cream.

Country lamb

C · O · U · N · T · D · O · W · N

On the day:

Prepare the vegetables.

To serve at 1 pm:

11.00: Open the red wine.

12.15: Cube and sauté the lamb. Prepare and add the remaining ingredients, cover and simmer for about 30 minutes.

12.30: Make up the Ginger Orange Trifle and decorate with the whipped cream and orange slices. Cover and refrigerate.

12.40: Scrub about 750 g/1½ lb new potatoes and cook. Prepare and cook the carrots (see introduction).

12.50: Heat the asparagus, drain and arrange on dishes. Fry the eggs.

1.00: Transfer the potatoes, carrots and lamb to serving dishes, cover and keep warm. Top the asparagus with the eggs, melted butter and Parmesan, then serve with wholemeal (wholewheat) rolls.

F · R · E · E · Z · E · R · N · O · T · E · S

Cool, pack and freeze the Country Lamb at the end of stage 3. Thaw overnight in the refrigerator. Bring to the boil, cover and simmer for 10 to 15 minutes, adding more stock if necessary. Stir in the mint and finish as per recipe.

I · N · D · E · X

A·C·K·N·O·W·L·E·D·G·E·M·E·N·T·S

Bryce Atwell 19, 51; The Banana Group 7, 59; British Chicken Information Service 15; Butter Information Council Ltd 23, 31, 39, 47, 54, 63; Robert Golden 10, 34; Christine Hanscomb 43; Charlie Stebbings 27.

Jacket photography: Clive Streeter   Illustration: Sally Davies